M000214563

The Family Book of Midrash

The Family Book of Midrash

52 *Jewish Stories from the Sages*

BARBARA DIAMOND GOLDIN

ROWMAN & LITTLEFIELD PUBLISHERS, INC.
Lanham • Boulder • New York • Toronto • Plymouth, UK

ROWMAN & LITTLEFIELD PUBLISHERS, INC.

Published in the United States of America
by Rowman & Littlefield Publishers, Inc.
A wholly owned subsidiary of The Rowman & Littlefield Publishing Group, Inc.
4501 Forbes Boulevard, Suite 200, Lanham, Maryland 20706
www.rowmanlittlefield.com

Estover Road
Plymouth PL6 7PY
United Kingdom

Copyright © 1990 by Barbara Diamond Goldin
First Rowman & Littlefield edition published in 2006

All rights reserved. No part of this publication may be reproduced,
stored in a retrieval system, or transmitted in any form or by any
means, electronic, mechanical, photocopying, recording, or otherwise,
without the prior permission of the publisher.

British Library Cataloguing in Publication Information Available

The hardback edition of this book was previously cataloged by the Library of Congress as
follows:

Goldin, Barbara Diamond.
  The family book of Midrash : 52 Jewish stories from the sages / Barbara Goldin.
    p. cm.
  Includes bibliographical references.
  Summary: Presents stories of heroic individuals from the Talmud and Midrash.
    1. Legends, Jewish—Juvenile literature. [1. Midrash—Juvenile literature. 2.
Aggada—Juvenile literature. 3. Folklore, Jewish. 4. Midrash. 5. Aggada.] I. Title.
BM530.G54 1991
296.1'420521—dc20   90-39598
ISBN-13: 978-0-7425-5285-2 (pbk. : alk. paper)
ISBN-10: 0-7425-5285-3 (pbk. : alk. paper)

Printed in the United States of America

♾™ The paper used in this publication meets the minimum requirements of American
National Standard for Information Sciences—Permanence of Paper for Printed Library
Materials, ANSI/NISO Z39.48-1992.

For my daughter,
Josee Sarah,
who is a lover of stories
and carries many within her.

Contents

Acknowledgment

Besides delving into the books that contained these stories, I also relied on people as resources in writing this collection. My appreciation goes to my editor, Arthur Kurzweil, who answered my questions with patience, knowledge, resourcefulness, and friendship. And to Muriel Jorgensen and the staff of Jason Aronson, Inc., who saw the book through to its publication.

Rabbi Edward Friedman fielded many of my questions about Talmud and primary source material. Sondra Botnick guided me through the wealth of Jewish books in her store, The Jewish Bookfinder. Rabbi Gershon Winkler, Dr. Judith Hauptman, and Ellen Frankel helped me in my search for more stories about women. I am grateful to Rabbi Daniel and Hanna Tiferet Siegel for introducing me to midrash and for transmitting their enthusiasm for Jewish learning and spiritual growth. And to Jane Yolen, who has inspired and guided my growth as a writer.

I am also thankful to the people who listened to each of these fifty-two stories and gave me valuable feedback for revisions. To the people in my writing groups: Amy, Chris, Connie, Cornelia, Dennis, Dixie, Ellen, Gloria, Helen, Lauren, Mary L., Mary M., and Peg; and to my children, Jeremy and Josee. And to Alan for his support during the three years it took me to complete this book.

Introduction

This collection gives the reader a taste of the thousands of stories one can find in the treasure house of rabbinic literature. Some of these stories are humorous, some mysterious, some tense with drama or adventure, some filled with the joy of a miracle and the beauty of faith. Some are about a kind merchant or a poor fisherman, others about famous kings and rabbis. There are stories about what a family does with a treasure they discover in their backyard, how something can be both good and evil, what it was like for Noah on the ark trying to determine what each animal ate.

Within these stories, children will find heroic individuals who are just as brave and daring as the current ones who sport masks and capes and carry fancy weapons. They will meet people like Rabbi Johanan Ben Zakkai, who escaped the besieged city of Jerusalem in a coffin, or Rabbi Akiva, who continued to teach Torah despite the harsh Roman laws forbidding it. But these rabbinic heroes provide something many of the cartoon heroes do not—moral and ethical values as a basis for action.

All of these stories come from either the Talmud or the Midrash. The Talmud is made up of two works—the Mishnah, which was written down about 200 C.E., and the Gemara, compiled in about 500 C.E. In the Mishnah, the rabbis of the time discuss the laws and passages found in the Bible and expound on its events and characters. The Gemara is further commentary on the Mishnah.

The second source for the stories is the post-talmudic body of writings called Midrash, which includes works such as *Midrash Rabbah* and *Pirke de Rabbi Eliezer*. In broader terms, the word *midrash* has come to mean a Jewish story that explains, clarifies, or elaborates on an event or passage in the Bible. The word itself

comes from the root *derash*, which means "to search out," "to expound," or "to examine."

The Talmud and Midrash are part of the Oral Law, whereas the Bible is called the Written Law. The tradition considers both Written and Oral Law sacred and given by God to Moses on Mount Sinai.

In the process of retelling, I have kept close to the original stories, yet used language and imagery that would appeal to contemporary children and adults. Also, I relied heavily on background research into the times and lives of the people in the stories to fill in the often very brief original stories with detail, history, dialogue, and scenes to make them easier to understand. While avoiding didactic retelling, I have tried to preserve the values, beliefs, and messages inherent in the original stories.

My goal has been to make these stories from Talmud and Midrash accessible to today's children, ages 8 and up, regardless of their background in Judaism. A story such as "Solomon and the Demon King" can now captivate a fifth grader who plays computer games and rides a skateboard just as much as it did a shtetl boy who walked barefoot to *cheder* (school) and learned to chant talmudic passages at age 4.

When choosing which stories to retell, I did not attempt to cover every famous biblical character or event, or to include one story about each sage. Rather, I chose those stories with strong plots that would appeal the most to the reader. At the same time, I made an effort to include stories about women, such as "The Women's Reward" and "Alexander's Lesson," and to keep the God language non–gender-specific.

I hope this collection will show that the stories the rabbis told are not old and outdated, but alive and timeless, and that they can be tapped for our children's enjoyment just as they were for the children of the generations that preceded us.

THE
FAMILY
BOOK
OF
MIDRASH

The Animals in the Ark

Building the ark was a big job for Noah, but loading the ark with two of each kind of animal was an even bigger job. The most difficult job of all, however, was feeding the animals.

There were so many different kinds of animals in the ark, and each one had to be fed a particular kind of food. This one ate hay, that one berries; this one grains, that one meat. Some animals ate in the daytime and others only at night.

Day and night, Noah and his wife and their three sons and their sons' wives were busy feeding the animals. Often they did not even have time to feed themselves.

Sometimes an animal became ill and needed special attention, like the lion who developed a fever. And sometimes an animal would not eat the food Noah put in front of it. This was the case with the little chameleons.

Noah gave them berries.

But the chameleons did not touch them.

Noah offered seeds and grasses.

The chameleons didn't touch these either.

He gave them leaves, and straw, and meat, but still the little chameleons wouldn't eat them and they grew pale and smaller.

Noah worried about the little chameleons. He was afraid they might die. Often he would stand by the lizards and talk softly to them.

"If only you could tell me what you need," he would say.

But the chameleons said nothing, because, of course, they cannot speak as humans do.

One day when Noah came to see the chameleons, he was carrying a pomegranate with him, intending to eat it. With all the animals braying and cackling, screeching and howling for their

food, Noah just grabbed what he could for himself and ate wherever he stood.

Noah suddenly noticed a little hole in the pomegranate and sure enough, as he sliced around it, a little worm wiggled out and fell to the floor. Immediately, the chameleons came to life. They raced forward, flicking their tongues, and caught the worm and ate it.

Noah was delighted. "Now I know what to feed you, little ones."

From then on, Noah saved any food that grew wormy for the chameleons and they grew healthy. Their green and blue scales shone brightly again.

Noah and his family continued to feed and take care of all the animals until the rains ended and the waters receded. When at last he and his family and all the creatures left the ark, Noah felt a great relief. No longer would he be responsible for feeding all these animals. Now they could find their own food in God's world—in the forests, the fields, the swamps, and the dry places.

Sanhedrin 108b

How Dishonesty Entered the Ark

N oah stood by the ark that he had built at God's command, helping all the living creatures board. They boarded in pairs, a male and a female from each species.

Along with the lions and tigers, eagles and cranes, butterflies and lizards came Dishonesty, a shadowy, nearly transparent figure.

Dishonesty crept alongside the lizards toward the boat.

"Wait!" cried Noah. "I see you there! You can't just slip in like that."

"And why not?" grumbled Dishonesty.

"No creature may enter the ark without a proper mate, a partner," answered Noah.

"Is that so?" queried Dishonesty, and slunk away, looking for a mate.

It passed many creatures large and small, running, flying, jumping, and hopping toward the ark.

"Will you be my mate?" Dishonesty asked the gazelle.

"I have a mate," answered gazelle.

"Will you be my mate?" Dishonesty asked the bluebird.

"My mate flies with me," said bluebird.

"Will you be my mate?" Dishonesty asked the rabbit.

Rabbit just laughed and hopped off with its mate.

By this time, Dishonesty was worried, for so many creatures were boarding the ark, each with a partner, and it had none. Nearly desperate, Dishonesty finally spotted a small, wiry figure digging all alone around a tree.

Dishonesty ran to the small figure.

"Where did you come from?" asked the digger, whose name was Trouble.

"From Noah," said Dishonesty. "I wanted to enter the ark, but Noah wouldn't let me unless I had a mate. Would you come with me and be my mate? Then together we can escape the flood."

"What flood?" said Trouble. "And anyway, can't you see I'm busy uprooting this tree?"

"You and that tree will be covered with water unless you listen to me."

"I don't believe you for a minute," said Trouble and turned back to the tree.

"Don't you see all the animals running that way to the ark?" pointed out Dishonesty.

Trouble reconsidered. "Well, if I do come, what will you give me?"

"Give you?" Dishonesty could not believe Trouble. "A flood is coming. There's no time to chat and strike bargains."

Trouble stood firm. "What will you give me if I come with you?"

"All right, then," answered Dishonesty. "Everything that comes to me you may take."

So Dishonesty and Trouble ran back to the ark. "I have found a proper mate," Dishonesty called to Noah. "Now you must let me come on board."

Hand in hand, they walked onto the ark, in between the worms and the crocodiles. With the lions and tigers, eagles and cranes,

butterflies and lizards, they too entered the world of the rainbow, of Noah and his family.

And this is how Dishonesty and Trouble survived the great flood that covered the earth. And this is how, in this world, it came to be that the harder Dishonesty worked, the richer Trouble became.

Midrash Psalms 7:11

Pharaoh's Crown

When Moses was a little boy, he was very much loved by Pharaoh's daughter and lived with her in the palace. She would hug and kiss him as if he were her own son.

Pharaoh, the King of Egypt, also played with him. Sometimes Moses would take the crown off Pharaoh's head and put it on his.

One day, when Moses was three years old, he was playing with the Pharaoh and reached for his crown. Balaam, a prince of Egypt, saw this and became terrified!

"Pharaoh! Don't you remember what your counselors said? They prophesied that one day someone will come and take your crown and your kingdom! See how Moses wears your crown now! This may be a sign that he is the one who will also take your kingdom."

Pharaoh grew afraid at Balaam's words and called a meeting of his counselors. One of the advisors who came was not really a counselor of Egypt, but the angel Gabriel in disguise.

After the counselors heard Balaam speak, they were also afraid that what Moses had done was a sign of the prophecy.

"Surely he will be the one to take away your kingdom," one said. "He must be killed."

When the other counselors agreed that Moses should be killed, the angel Gabriel spoke up.

"Moses is only a little boy," he explained. "Taking Pharaoh's crown does not mean that Moses will take Pharaoh's kingdom.

"Let us give him a test. By putting a piece of gold and a glowing coal in front of him, we will be able to determine his intentions.

"If he reaches for the gold, we will know that he understands its value, as well as the meaning of Pharaoh's crown. If so, he shall die.

"If he reaches for the coal, we will know that he has only the sense of a little boy and took Pharaoh's crown as a plaything. Then he shall live."

The counselors agreed to the test.

As the servant placed the shiny gold piece and the glowing coal in front of Moses, the great hall became silent and the people in attendance waited and watched anxiously.

Little Moses lifted his hand to reach for the bright gold piece, but as he did, the angel Gabriel thrust Moses' hand aside so quickly that no one saw him move. In this way he forced Moses to seize the coal instead.

As children do, Moses put the glowing object in his mouth. It was so hot that it burned his tongue, and because of this, he would have difficulty speaking all the rest of his days. But he did pass Pharaoh's test, and when he grew up he became the leader who would take his people, Israel, out of Egypt.

Midrash Rabbah Exodus 1:26

Moses' Staff

When Moses was a young man, he had to flee Egypt in fear for his life. In his wanderings, he came to the city of Midian, to a well that shepherds used. At the well, there was much bickering and teasing between the shepherds and a group of young women.

Moses went to aid the women. He chased away the shepherds and watered the sheep that belonged to the women.

"We are the daughters of the priest Jethro," one explained. "Ever since our father stopped serving idols, things have not gone well for us. The shepherds refuse to care for our flocks, so my father must depend on us, his daughters."

Moses listened sympathetically. He liked these daughters of the priest Jethro, and especially this one named Zipporah.

"Sometimes we fill the troughs with water and the shepherds

push us away," she continued. "They let their own flocks drink from it. And today they threatened to throw us into the well." She looked up at Moses and added, "We are grateful to you for your help."

"I would be glad to walk with you," said Moses. "To be sure you arrive home safely."

Moses helped Zipporah and her sisters shepherd the flocks to their home. Never had he met a woman such as Zipporah before. She spoke well, with courage and sensitivity, and carried herself proudly. Moses knew that she was the woman he wanted to marry.

"I have looked for someone like you in all my travels," Moses said to Zipporah. "Would you consider becoming my wife?"

Zipporah stopped walking and studied Moses' face. "You decide things quickly, my friend," she said. "But even if I wanted to, it could not come to be. My father insists that the man who wishes to marry one of his daughters must uproot the tree that grows in our garden."

"Is it such a big tree that I cannot uproot it?" asked Moses.

"It is not so big," said Zipporah. "But it has the power to swallow anyone who tries to touch it."

"I have never heard of such a tree," said Moses in disbelief.

"I know," said Zipporah. "This tree is really a rod carved with the name of the Holy One and other secret symbols. God created it from the sapphire on the divine throne itself, in the twilight of the first Sabbath evening.

"God gave it to Adam who passed it on to Enoch and then to Noah, Shem, Abraham, Isaac, and finally Jacob. Jacob brought it to Egypt and gave it to his son Joseph. When Joseph died, the Egyptians stole the rod and brought it to Pharaoh's palace.

"My father was a scribe at the palace then. When he saw the rod, he was awed by its beauty and holiness and took it for himself.

"My father carried the rod here when he came to Midian many years ago. When walking in the garden one day, he absentmindedly stuck it into the ground. As much as he tried, he could not pull it out again. Before his eyes, it budded and blossomed into a tree.

"And so he tests every man who tries to marry one of us. He says the man who pulls the rod out will be the man who will lead the Hebrews out of Egypt."

Zipporah lowered her voice. "It is no use, Moses. Do not even try."

Moses and Zipporah walked together in silence the rest of the way to Jethro's house.

Jethro was surprised to see his daughters return from the well so soon.

"You finished early today," he said.

"This kind man helped us," answered Zipporah.

In appreciation, Jethro invited Moses into his home to eat and drink. After the meal, Moses told Jethro how much he cared for his daughter Zipporah. "I would like to marry her," he said.

"If you can fetch the rod growing as a tree in my garden," Jethro said, "then I shall give Zipporah to you."

Moses nodded.

Zipporah led him to the garden and showed him the tree. "I wish you would not try to do this," she said.

"This tree looks just like any other tree," Moses responded.

As Moses touched the trunk of the tree, however, he could feel it moving, pulling him, sucking him into its very marrow. But Moses did not let go.

He said to himself, "You are a Prince of Egypt, a descendant of Joseph and Jacob before him. Of Isaac and Abraham, Shem, Noah, Enoch, and Adam."

Feeling God's strength flow through him, Moses pulled and pulled on that trunk, all the while that it pulled him. He struggled with the rod-tree for what seemed like hours. Zipporah, Jethro, and all the others who had gathered around did not say a word. They just watched to see who would win—the tree or Moses.

The two seemed an even match. The struggle went on until it was almost dark, and Moses had little energy left. He summoned what strength he could and concentrated his energy one last time. He could feel the rod-tree's roots loosen from the earth.

Moses pulled until he freed the entire tree. As he held it in the air above him, it became a rod in his hands, a rod that gleamed sapphire blue in the sunlight. He could see the engravings of the Holy letters of the name of God on the rod, as well as other mysterious letters whose meaning he did not know.

Moses brought the ancient rod to Jethro.

"As I have promised, I give you my daughter Zipporah to marry," said Jethro. "I give you the rod also. May it serve you well."

And so the rod that God created in the twilight of the first Sabbath eve was passed on to Moses the prophet, who would lead his people out of Egypt.

It would be the very rod he would use in Egypt to work the miracles. For the mysterious letters on the rod spelled out the

initials of the names of the ten plagues that God would inflict on the Egyptians to convince Pharaoh to let the Hebrews go.

Midrash Rabbah Exodus 1:30–32, 8:3
Midrash Va Yosha 42–44
Pirke de Rabbi Eliezer 40

Why God Chose Mount Sinai

All of creation heard the news—the birds and the winds, the rivers and the mountains. Soon God would give the gift of the Ten Commandments to Moses on top of a mountain. But no one knew which mountain it would be.

Every mountain wished to be chosen. Every mountain had good reasons.

"God should definitely choose me." As Mount Tabor spoke, its sides shuddered and quaked, waking up the night animals and shaking leaves off the bushes. "I am the highest mountain. When God sent the great flood, I was the only mountain that was not covered by water. Noah and his ark rested on *me* while waiting for the rains to end and the waters to recede."

"That may be so," put in Mount Carmel. "But if it were not for me, the Israelites could not have crossed the Red Sea. The Egyptians were behind them and the sea in front of them. They would have been caught and enslaved again in the land of Egypt."

Mount Carmel puffed up its sides, causing the snakes and lizards, the deer and wild goats to go rolling into the ravines and gulleys. "But I came to their rescue. I put myself down in the middle of the sea so the Israelites could cross on top of me to the other side. God should definitely choose me."

Mount Zion joined in the quarrel. And so did Mount Herman. Each mountain's argument sounded strong and just.

Only little Mount Sinai remained quiet.

Why should God chose me? Mount Sinai thought. I am the

smallest of all the mountains and I have never done anything great at all.

The argument continued far into the night. No animal found any rest, no bird a quiet spot. Even the trees and flowers became annoyed with the bickering:

"It should be me!"

"No. I deserve . . . ."

"If it weren't for . . . ."

"I'll be the one chosen."

Suddenly a voice that came from nowhere—yet from everywhere—silenced the mountains.

"Enough boasting!" said God. "I have made my decision!"

The mountains became quiet. All listened eagerly—the birds and animals, the trees and flowers. Which mountain would God choose for the great gift? Mount Tabor or Mount Carmel? Mount Zion or Mount Herman?

"It will be on the smallest and most humble of mountains that I will give my gift," God continued. "On little Mount Sinai."

The four mountains gasped and moaned (at least as well as such great masses of rocks and soil can gasp and moan).

"I never expected . . . ."

"Who would have thought . . . ."

"Why should such a . . . ."

But the animals and birds filled the air with happy twittering sounds, because they were so tired of the roaring and quaking and boasting.

And little Mount Sinai glowed from top to bottom.

Midrash Psalms 68:9

The Most Precious Gift

God wants to give us a gift, the Torah," Moses told the Israelites one day while they were camped in the desert. "Will you accept this gift without knowing what it is or what you must do once you accept it?"

The people crowded around Moses, somewhat bewildered. Then someone spoke up.

"God gave us our freedom! Of course we should accept any gift that comes from God."

There were many shouts of agreement among the people.

Moses smiled. "Then I will go up the mountain and tell God you will accept the Torah, God's teachings, even though you do not know what it asks of you."

For days, the people watched for Moses' return, hoping to see God's gift.

What is this Torah? they all wondered. Is it small enough to fit in Moses' hands? Could it be more wonderful than the well that never ran dry, or the food from heaven that they ate each day?

The time went by slowly.

Finally, cheers and cries of excitement spread through the camp.

"I see him!"

"That moving speck coming down the mountain!"

"There's Moses!"

The people gathered to greet Moses. But their excitement vanished as he came closer. He carried nothing in his hands and there was no smile on his face.

"Where's the gift?" they all asked.

Moses waited until the people quieted.

"I told God what you said," Moses began. "That you would accept the Torah even though you do not know what is in it."

All the people nodded in agreement.

"But God wants an assurance from us that we will not only accept this gift but will keep it and live by it. God wants us to give something as a guarantee."

The people were quiet.

What could we give God to show we mean what we say? What is most precious to us? they wondered.

The sun sparkling on an earring gave someone an idea.

"Our jewels! They are our most valuable possessions!"

Shouts of agreement rang through the camp as everyone took off earrings and bracelets, necklaces and rings, and placed them on the growing pile before Moses.

Moses gathered the jewelry into a large sack, which he placed on his shoulders, and slowly made his way up the mountain.

Again the people waited. Days and days went by until the noisy bustle of the camp was broken by cries of excitement.

"He's coming!"

"I see him!"

Once again the people gathered to greet Moses. But once again they were disappointed.

"No Torah?" they asked.

"No," answered Moses. "I offered God all our jewelry—our earrings and bracelets, necklaces and rings. But God wants something more from us, something that will give assurance that we will keep the Torah and live by it."

What could be more precious, more valuable than jewelry? the people wondered.

Then someone had an idea.

"We have other things in the camp more precious to us than jewelry," he said. "A box carved by my father. A cloth carefully woven in colors of the sea and the sunset. Perhaps God would accept these as a guarantee."

The people scattered to their tents to find a gift for God, and another pile grew before Moses.

He gathered the gifts, each one unique, each one beautiful, and began his climb.

The people were hopeful, for they had given Moses those things most precious to them. They sang as they tended the animals and cleaned the camp.

The days passed until someone caught sight of Moses returning down the mountain path.

The singing stopped. His arms were empty.

"God liked our gifts," Moses explained. "But God said that a piece of cloth, no matter how carefully worked, will not guarantee that we will follow the Torah. We must offer something else."

The people were stunned by Moses' words. What could they offer God besides jewelry and gifts?

It was then that a mother with a baby on her hip spoke up.

"Jewelry and gifts are not our most precious possession," she said. Everyone in the camp turned to listen. "Our children are. Perhaps we could assure God we will keep the Torah by teaching it to our children. Perhaps that could be our guarantee."

"You are right," the people agreed. "Whatever is in the Torah, we will teach to our children."

This time when Moses climbed the mountain, he carried no sack, but only the people's promise.

Each day the people looked out for Moses. When he returned they could see that he carried something in his hands—two large stone tablets that shone with the words of God.

They shouted. They danced and sang. They gathered to greet Moses and see this gift, the Torah, that he held so lovingly in his hands.

Moses' face shone with the same light as the words on the tablets.

"God has accepted our guarantee," he told them, "and given us the Torah. It will teach us how to live as a free people in our new land. Its stories and laws will fill our hearts and surround us with light."

And so the children of Israel listened to the words of the Torah and learned them. Keeping their word, they taught the Torah to their children, passing the light from one generation to another, to this very day.

Midrash Rabbah Song of Songs 1:4

Moses Visits Akiva

When Moses received the Torah, the law, from God on Mount Sinai, he noticed that God placed three small lines on the top of some of the letters, as if these letters were being crowned.

"Oh, Holy One," asked Moses, "why do You crown these letters?"

"I do this because of a teacher named Akiva ben Joseph, who will live in the land of Israel over a thousand years from now. He will teach his students about every letter, even every crown of every letter, in the Torah."

"If I could but see this great teacher once," wished Moses aloud, "I could learn the secrets of these crowns."

"Turn around," answered God.

Moses stood up and did as God commanded.

As he turned, the force of the wind made his eyes close. Then he felt the crisp cool air of the mountaintop change to the warm, musty air of a crowded room. The quiet of the mountain also changed. Now came the noise of people speaking and moving about.

Slowly Moses opened his eyes. He was startled to find himself in the back of a large room filled with people seated in rows, all facing a strong, tall man who was speaking.

So this is Akiva ben Joseph, thought Moses.

Moses sat for a long while in Akiva's classroom, listening.

It was true; Rabbi Akiva did speak about every letter and every crown of every letter written in the Torah. His students asked questions and Akiva answered them. But Moses grew more and more uncomfortable in Akiva's classroom, for he could not make sense of these discussions.

Akiva's teachings are beyond my understanding, thought Moses. Why didn't God choose someone else, someone like Akiva, to receive the Torah, someone who could understand all it has to teach. There is so much I do not know.

Then something Akiva said to a student surprised Moses in this far away time and place. His face brightened and his eyes grew lively again.

"I know this," Akiva said, "because it is a law revealed to Moses on Mount Sinai."

"Moses." His own name echoed in his ears and grew louder and louder from a whisper to a call. "Moses!"

He knew now that he had a place in this long line of receiving and teaching Torah. And that even though he did not understand all the mysteries of the Torah—all the mysteries of its letters and crowns as Akiva did—God had still asked him to climb the mountain and receive the law.

Moses felt grateful as he closed his eyes, and turned once again to feel the crisp cool air of the mountaintop play against his face.

"I am ready, Holy One," he said, "to bring the letters and the crowns, the words and the laws to the people."

Menahot 29b

The Women's Reward

When Moses left the Israelites at the base of Mount Sinai, he told them, "I will return in forty days to bring you God's words, the Torah."

The people counted the days until they would see their leader again. Forty days seemed like such a long time to wait. And it was.

Finally, the fortieth day came. At noon on that day, the people saw a false and terrifying vision. Midway between heaven and earth

floated the dead body of their leader on a burial platform. Waves of shock and sorrow reverberated through the camp.

"It's real," said one Israelite.

"Our leader is dead," bemoaned another.

The people pointed and wept. They felt alone in this vast, unfamiliar desert and grew more and more afraid.

Suddenly someone shouted from the crowd that gathered around Aaron, Moses' brother. "We need a god like the Egyptians'."

"One we can see. One we can dance and sing to, and carry with us through the desert."

"One that will protect us from the snakes and scorpions and wild animals."

"Let us make a calf like the Egyptians have!"

But people now began pushing and shoving one another, because not everyone agreed.

"Can't we wait one more day?"

"Perhaps Moses did not count the day he ascended the mountain when he told us forty days."

"No. We've waited long enough."

"Moses will not return. A golden calf is what we need."

The arguing went back and forth, all around the camp. Aaron stood in the middle.

I will let the argument go on, he thought. Perhaps if it goes on long enough, it will give Moses time to return.

But the people who wanted the idol grew stronger and louder. They pressured Aaron with their presence and their words, their pushing and their fears.

What else can I do to hold off these people? Aaron thought, afraid of what would happen to them if they killed him in their haste to make themselves a god. Who, then, would watch over them until Moses returned? For Aaron knew in his heart that Moses would return.

He looked over the crowd and saw that the women stayed back, while the men demanded that the idol be made.

I will ask the women for their gold jewelry to make the idol and they will refuse, Aaron thought. Perhaps by then Moses will have returned.

"Women of the camp!" shouted Aaron. "Give me your earrings and bracelets and neck ornaments to make this golden calf!"

As he suspected, the women refused to give him their jewelry.

And when their husbands demanded the jewels, the women still refused.

"A calf of gold has no power," they told their husbands.

But still Moses did not come.

So the men tore off their own earrings, which they wore in the fashion of the Egyptians, and insisted that Aaron melt these to make a calf they could worship.

It did not take them long to make the idol. When Moses descended the mountain with the two tablets of stone the next day, he saw his people worshiping a golden calf. In his anger, he threw the first set of tablets down and they shattered on the rocks.

He strode into the middle of the camp and said, "Whoever is on God's side, come to me."

The whole tribe of Levi went to stand by Moses. Others followed.

Then Moses took the golden calf and burned it in the fire. A great punishment fell on those men who had kissed the calf—the punishment of death.

But the women were not punished, for they had refused to take part in the making of the idol. As a reward, God gave them the New Moon holiday, called Rosh Hodesh, to be celebrated throughout the generations.

At each appearance of the new moon, the women would stop work, sing blessings, share festive meals with their sisters, light candles, and dance with the Shekhinah, God's presence in the world.

Each appearance of the new moon would bring them the kind of refreshment that is food and rest for the spirit as well as for the body.

Exodus 32:1–35
Midrash Rabbah Numbers 21:10
Pirke de Rabbi Eliezer, chap. 45

The Widow's Gold

In the time of Saul, King of Israel, there lived a wealthy man who had a beautiful wife. Since the man was much older than his wife, she was still young and beautiful when he died.

The governor of the province had long desired this woman and her riches, and decided that this was his chance to marry her. But the widow disliked the greedy, pompous governor, and did not want to marry him at all.

I must leave my home, the widow thought, for neither my gold nor I am safe here while the governor lives.

The widow devised a plan to hide her gold. She placed all her coins in clay jars and poured in honey to cover them. Then, after asking a good friend of her husband to store the honey jars, she fled from the city.

The friend did not touch the widow's jars in his keeping until the day of his son's wedding. On that day, the cooks used so much honey that they did not have enough to finish making the sweet cakes.

The friend remembered the clay jars in his cellar.

There would be no harm in my using some of the widow's honey, he thought. Tomorrow I can buy more and refill the jars.

With his lamp, the friend went into his cellar and began to scoop honey from one of the jars. As his bowl filled, he noticed something shiny slide in with the honey.

He looked closer and then pulled out the object.

That's odd, he thought. Why is there a gold coin in here?

He held the lamp over the mouth of the jar and saw many more gold coins covered with the sticky honey.

Quickly, he checked the other jars. They too were filled with honey and gold coins.

In his greed at seeing so much gold, the man forgot his friendship with the widow's husband. He emptied all the coins from the jars. After his son's wedding, he filled the jars again—with honey.

The widow might be clever, he thought, but I can be just as clever as she.

After a time, the evil governor died. When the widow learned the news, she returned immediately to the city.

She greeted her husband's friend and asked him to return her jars.

"Certainly," he replied. "I will ask my servants to bring them to you."

When the widow was alone with her jars, she opened one to check the contents. All she found was honey.

"This can't be," she cried.

She looked in the next jar and the next. With each jar, the widow grew angrier and angrier, for in each one she found only honey.

"That thief!" The widow cried and wailed, and vowed to get her money back.

She returned to her husband's friend and demanded her gold coins.

"What coins?" the man answered. "You gave me jars filled with honey and I returned jars filled with honey."

Knowing now that her husband's friend would never willingly return her coins, she went to the judge of the city.

The judge was gentle and soft-spoken. After listening to her story, he asked, "Did anyone see you put your gold coins in the jars?"

"No," said the widow. "I wanted to hide them so no one would be tempted to take them. I covered the coins completely and told everyone that the jars were filled with honey."

"If there are no witnesses, then there is no way I can help you," the judge said. "Go to King Saul. Perhaps he can find a way."

So the widow went to see the King.

After hearing her story, the King called a meeting of the Sanhedrin, the highest court in Israel.

"Did anyone see you put the coins in the jars?" asked the judges.

"No. There was no one," answered the widow.

"Did you tell anyone that you were giving your gold to this friend for safekeeping?"

"No. No one," answered the widow. "I wanted to hide the coins in the honey to protect them from the governor and anyone else who might want my wealth."

"We are very sorry," said the judges. "We can only judge if there are witnesses. We cannot know what is truly in a person's heart."

Tearfully, the widow left the court.

Who will help me now? she wondered. Even the King and the Sanhedrin could not help me get back my gold.

As she walked, she cried.

A shepherd boy playing with his friends nearby saw her.

"What's the matter?" he asked her kindly. "Has someone hurt you?"

The widow told the boy about the jars and the gold, the theft and the judging.

"What is there for me to do now?" she cried softly, her head in her hands.

"Do this," said the boy. "Go to the King. Ask him to give me the authority in your case."

The widow, glad for any help, ran to the King.

"My Lord King," she said, "there is a shepherd boy who requests your permission to examine my case."

King Saul chuckled. "There is a boy who can do what the city court and the Sanhedrin could not? Bring him to me."

The shepherd boy appeared before the King.

"So you are the one who thinks he can decide this case?" the King asked.

"With God's help," answered the boy.

"What is your name?" asked the King.

"David," said the boy.

"Well, David, let us see what you can do."

David went to the widow's house and sent for her husband's friend.

"Are you sure these are the very jars you gave this man for safekeeping?" he asked the widow.

"Yes, these are my jars," she answered. "Except that my coins are missing from them."

"Do you agree that these are the same jars this widow gave you for safekeeping?" David asked the friend.

"Yes, these are the same jars," the man agreed. "The ones that were filled with honey."

"Then bring me some empty jars and we will transfer all the honey from these jars to the empty ones."

In front of the large crowd that had gathered at the widow's house, David poured the honey from the widow's jars into the empty ones. Next, to everyone's amazement, he smashed every one of the widow's jars into little pieces. He carefully searched through the broken pieces. When he found what he had been looking for, he stood up. In his hand were two gold coins.

"These two coins were stuck to the side of one of the widow's jars. They are proof that she did put gold coins and not only honey into these jars."

David turned to the husband's friend. "Return the coins that you have stolen from this widow. Every one," he said.

The man returned the coins. News of David's actions spread throughout the land of Israel, impressing even the King. One day, this same David would himself be King of Israel, as wise and as trusting in God as when he was a shepherd boy.

Yalkut Sippurim

David and the Spiderweb

O ne day, when David, King of Israel, was still a shepherd boy, he sat and watched a spider spin its web.

Why did God create such a creature, he wondered, a creature that spins what no one can wear?

As he grew up and went to live in King Saul's court, David forgot his curiosity about the spiderweb. But he remembered it years later when he had to escape from the King.

King Saul had grown jealous of David. Everyone in the palace loved the handsome, brave, and sensible David. Everyone in the land sang his praises.

Even Saul's own son Jonathan treated David as a brother, and his daughter Michal married him.

Perhaps David wishes to be King himself, Saul thought, and take the throne away from me.

He put David in charge of battles, hoping each time that the enemy would kill him. But each time, David emerged the victor.

The King no longer tried to hide his jealousy from the court. Jonathan knew of it and so did Michal. They feared for David's life.

Very late one night, Saul called for two of his guards.

"Go in secret to David's house," he ordered. "Keep watch and kill him in the morning."

Though the guards moved quietly around David's house, his wife, Michal, could sense the danger.

She woke her husband.

"David, run for your life tonight, or you will be killed," she told him. She pointed to the window. "This way," she whispered. "There are men by the door."

David escaped through the window and crept quietly from the city.

When he felt safe enough, he broke into a run.

The border, he thought. The caves and the hills. That's where I must hide.

Early the next morning, the guards searched David's house and reported his disappearance to the King.

Saul was angry.

"Bring me six soldiers," he ordered. "I will lead the search for David myself."

King Saul and his soldiers set out immediately.

Meanwhile, David had reached the hills and stopped for a quick rest. Running for hours over the fields and brush had tired him. He leaned against a tree and took out the piece of bread Michal had given him.

He didn't realize he had fallen asleep until he heard the clatter of horses and men.

Quickly, his eyes searched the valley below. He spotted the mounted soldiers climbing rapidly up the hills.

"So soon!" David muttered as he looked about him. He knew if Saul caught him, he would kill him. No matter that I have no plots against him, David thought. The King is mad with jealousy.

David spied a small cave in the hill and crawled in. Better here than being caught like a goat scrambling among the bushes, he thought.

David crouched inside the cave, listening and waiting, praying that they hadn't seen him.

The soldiers and Saul climbed up the hill, leading their horses, and soon David could hear their steps and their talk and the clamor of their weapons.

The sound of their footsteps stopped in front of the cave.

"I will search the cave," offered a soldier, preparing to remove his sword so he could crawl inside.

"No need," said King Saul. "Let's not waste our time here while

David runs farther away from us. See?" Saul pointed to a spider's web that covered the cave's entrance. "If he had gone in there, he would have broken the web."

Saul and his men left to continue their search while David thanked God for sending the spider and its delicate web.

I remember a time when I thought this spider a useless creature, thought David. How wrong I was. The spider spins a web that no one can wear, but that saved my life. How precious is every one of God's creatures.

Alphabet of Ben Sira 24b
Targum Psalms 57:3

The Wind, the Widow, and Solomon

Once there was a widow who lived in a little house by the sea. Though she had very little, she still gave more than her share to charity. Each day she baked three loaves of bread. Two she gave to the poor, and one she kept for herself.

One day a beggar came to her door, wearing the tattered clothes of a seaman.

"My ship was wrecked in a storm and I lost everything. Do you have any food for a hungry man?" he said.

Gladly the widow gave the man one of the loaves of bread she had baked.

The beggar had barely gone, when there was another knock on the widow's door.

A second beggar stood outside, his clothes ripped and his face smeared with dirt.

"I've escaped the slave traders," he explained, "and am trying to find my way home. Please—some bread for a hungry man."

Gladly the widow gave him her second loaf.

She sat down at the table, knife in hand, to cut herself a slice of the third loaf, when there was another knock.

Never have I had so many people pass my house, she thought.

When she opened her door, the widow saw a third beggar standing there. His clothes were those of a prosperous merchant, though torn and soiled.

"I was robbed on the highway," said the man, his voice quivering. "They took all my belongings but I managed to get away alive. Do you have any food to spare for me?"

The widow felt sorry for the man. Even though she had only one loaf left, she gave it to him.

What will I do now? she wondered after he left. I gave away my last loaf and I am hungry. I have not yet had any breakfast.

The widow looked about in her kitchen to see if there was any flour left. There was none. So she went to her supply of winter wheat and filled a sack with the dry kernels.

I will have to grind some more flour, she thought.

She left her little house and went to the mill by the river near the sea. There she ground her wheat into flour and filled the sack with it.

On her way home, the winds off the sea picked up the poor widow and blew her about. She held on tightly to her sack and kept walking. But a great gust came and blew all around her, spinning her around, and carrying off her sack.

"Here I have fed three beggars with my bread and you come and take my flour!" she called out angrily to the wind.

Instead of returning home, the widow decided to go to King Solomon. She would present her case against the wind before him and the high court.

After a journey of several days, the widow came to the palace. She asked for an audience with the King and told him and the sages all about the three loaves of bread and the flour and the wind.

Then she asked, "Is it possible to conduct a trial against the wind for taking my flour? I am so poor and have so little, I cannot bear to lose even a sackful."

Just as she finished speaking, three merchants came bursting into the court carrying an open chest filled with gold coins.

"We wish to give these coins to the poor people of your land," they told Solomon.

"Why such a large sum?" asked the king, surprised by the strangers' gift.

"We were traveling in a ship filled with precious cargo not long ago, when there was a storm," they told him. "It threw our boat about and ripped a hole in the side. Water came pouring in, filling the boat. We tried to stuff the hole with rags and pieces of clay and even our own clothes. But whatever we tried to stuff in the hole, the winds tore away. Meanwhile the boat was sinking ever faster. We prayed to God. We promised that if we were saved from this awful storm, we would give all the money we had on board to charity.

"Suddenly, the waters stopped filling our boat. As the storm subsided we saw that something had filled up the hole."

"What was it?" asked Solomon.

"An old sack," the merchants explained.

"Please bring it to me," said the King.

So the merchants went back to their boat. When they returned with the sack, the widow cried out, "Why, that's my own sack that I filled with flour, the one the wind carried out to sea."

"Then this gold is rightly yours," said Solomon, "for the wind took your sack to save the lives of these merchants. And now it has returned it to you with your reward."

The widow thanked King Solomon and the merchants. Satisfied, she took her reward back to her little house by the sea.

There she continued her life as before, except that now she had no worries. And she continued to give more than her share to charity.

Mimekor Yisrael: Classical Jewish Folktales
Vol. 1: National Tales

The Tower in the Sea

One of Solomon's daughters was an extraordinary beauty. When Solomon consulted the stars for the man she would marry, he learned that her intended would be a very poor youth from a family of scribes and weavers.

"I will do what I can to prevent such a union," Solomon told his advisors.

So he ordered a tower built of stone overlooking the sea. He took his daughter and placed her there, where she was watched by seventy trusted servants and provided with stores of food and drink.

The princess grew lonely in the tower. Her main diversion was

to climb to the tower's roof and gaze at the sea. She watched the birds and the leaping fish and the changing colors of the sea.

She often thought, I would rather be wed to a poor man than trapped in this tower day after day. But my father will not listen to reason.

For the princess, each day was just like the one before. She ate. She slept. She read. She sewed. She chatted with the servants. And always, she climbed the stairs to stare at the sea below.

But one day she met with a surprise on the tower roof. For as she gazed at the sea, a huge bird came toward her carrying the carcass of a dead ox. It dropped the remains right at the princess's feet as if it were bringing her a gift.

The princess shuddered. The ox was no pretty sight, having been picked over by birds and other creatures.

Suddenly, a movement from inside the bones of the carcass startled the princess. She poked gingerly through the ox's ribs and saw the figure of a young man within. He was stretching and yawning as if waking from a long sleep.

"Who are you and what are you doing in there?" she asked the youth.

"I'm a Jew from the city of Acco," he answered, just as startled as the princess to find himself by the sea instead of in the desert. "I was traveling and had no place to sleep until I found the remains of an old ox. I crept inside for the night to keep warm, and I fell asleep. But how did I get to such a place as this?"

"A giant bird brought the carcass to this tower with you in it," the princess answered. "Here. Come to my quarters and wash yourself. Then I will give you food to eat and see that you are taken back to Acco."

"But who are you?" he asked.

"One of the daughters of the King," she answered and would say no more.

While the youth washed and dressed himself in the fresh clothes that the princess had found for him in the servants' quarters, she went to the food pantries and filled a bowl with meat and bread and dried fruit for him.

When she returned, she was astonished to see how handsome he looked all washed and dressed. And as she talked to him she also learned about his keen mind and gentle ways.

The princess never did send for the servant to bring the youth back to Acco. Instead he stayed with her in her quarters and married her.

Using his own blood for ink, he drew up a marriage contract. As he was a scribe by trade, he knew the wording of such things.

Then he read the betrothal agreement aloud, calling God and the two archangels, Michael and Gabriel, as the witnesses.

After some time had passed, the servants took to whispering among themselves. It was beyond belief, but they were sure that the princess was growing big with child.

"How can this be?" they asked one another. "No one has been allowed to enter the tower from the outside except the King."

They questioned the princess and soon learned the truth from her. Then the servants feared King Solomon's wrath when he heard the news. So they waited to tell him. But as the princess grew bigger with child, the servants grew more and more fearful that Solomon would arrive unexpectedly and discover the news for himself. So they called for him.

He arrived by ship and they told him what had happened.

Solomon asked to see his daughter.

"I am married to a most handsome, kind, and wise man, father," she explained. "A giant bird brought him to me hidden in an ox's carcass."

The princess brought her husband to meet the King, who agreed indeed on the youth's beauty and wisdom. He questioned the young man about his family and the place he was from.

"So you are from Acco," the King mused. "A scribe. And your father is a scribe. Your mother a weaver. You then are the youth the stargazers predicted would wed my daughter. So no matter what I tried to do, I could not prevent this union after all."

The princess frowned as she stared at her father. Was he very displeased with her? she wondered. He had great power, her father.

But the King smiled. As if reading her mind, he said, "Some things are more powerful than kings. Love. Destiny. The ways of the Holy One. May you two always be happy with each other."

So the King gave his blessing to the marriage and a prayer of thanks to God for his new son-in-law.

Tanhuma, Introduction
Exempla of the Rabbis, p. 136.

Solomon and the Demon King

Whfen King Solomon was rebuilding the Temple in Jerusalem, he had a problem. How could his workers cut and fit the stones from the quarry if the Torah prohibited the use of iron tools in the construction of the holy building? It is said that because iron is used to make implements of war, it cannot be used to build that which is holy.

Solomon met with the rabbis to discuss this problem.

"What am I to do without iron tools?" he asked.

The rabbis were quiet. Then one of them spoke up.

"There is a creature that Moses used to cut the names of the tribes in the precious stones of the high priest's breastplate. It is called a shamir and is a special worm that can split rocks."

"But how do I find such a creature?" asked Solomon.

"The demons know the whereabouts of the shamir," said the rabbi. "You must capture a male and a female demon, tie them together, and question them."

Solomon knew that demons, those spirits of the night who trouble people's minds and plague their souls, lurked in ruins and waste places.

So that night, before midnight, he sent his guards to an abandoned inn at the edge of the city. There they caught two demons, a male and a female, and tied them together. They brought them in a sack before Solomon.

As the demons tumbled out of the sack, a great coldness filled the hall.

The demons struggled to stand up. The larger one was covered with hair and had a tongue that reached down to his stomach. The smaller one was just as ugly, for she had long pointed ears and a snakelike tail.

King Solomon stood before the demons holding a stick of burning incense in his hand.

The demons, smelling the incense, stayed a respectful distance from Solomon, for they abhored such strong, sweet odors.

But they were angry.

"Why did you bring us here?" the hairy one shouted at Solomon in a high, rasping voice. "You'd better have good reason or . . . ." He turned to look at his companion, the two concocting mischief already.

"I intend to release you," said Solomon, "as soon as you tell me the whereabouts of the shamir."

The demon laughed an eerie laugh. "And why should we tell you anything?" he replied.

"If you chose not to," said Solomon, "I will keep you both locked up forever, never again free to roam the haunts or meet with other demons. And no demon will be able to reach you, for I have in my possession a ring bearing God's most secret name."

The two demons shuddered.

Finally, the smaller demon spoke up in a squeaky cackle. Her tail jumped up and down behind her with every word. "We know many things," she said. "But only the King of the Demons, Asmodeus, knows where the shamir is hidden."

"Where can I find Asmodeus?" said Solomon.

"He lives at the top of the farthermost mountain in your kingdom," she replied. "He always returns there when he is thirsty, for there is a well on the side of the mountain that he keeps covered with a large stone. He seals the stone every time he journeys from his home. On his return, he carefully checks the seal before opening the well and drinking the water."

Solomon thanked the demons for their help before releasing them. Then he chose his most trusted counselor and friend, Benaiahu, for the task of capturing Asmodeus.

Solomon told Benaiahu all that the demons had said. Then he handed his friend a chain and his ring engraved with the holy name of God, a bundle of wool, and bottles of wine. "Take these with you," he said. "You will find use for them."

By the time Benaiahu reached the farthermost mountain of Solomon's kingdom, he had devised a plan.

After he located Asmodeus's well, he dug a pit just below it. Then he dug a hole in the bottom of the well, so the water could flow down into the pit.

Benaiahu stopped up the hole with the wool Solomon had given him, and proceeded to dig another pit directly above the

well. Into this pit he poured wine and watched as it trickled down and filled the well.

Covering all traces of his work on the montainside, Benaiahu climbed a nearby tree to wait for the return of the Demon King.

When evening came, Benaiahu heard a great flapping sound. The giant demon Asmodeus hovered above the trees and then flew down through the air to his well.

Benaiahu watched as Asmodeus checked the seal. It was untouched.

The demon moved the stone aside easily and began to drink. To his astonishment, instead of cool, clear water, he tasted the heady sweetness of wine. Asmodeus drew back, puzzled. But he was very thirsty from his travels and could not resist for long. He drank and drank of the wine, until he fell into a drunken sleep.

Benaiahu jumped down and fastened the chain around the Demon King, sealing it with King Solomon's ring.

When Asmodeus finally awoke, he struggled to release himself from the chains.

"It is no use," said Benaiahu. "The name of God seals those chains. You of all creatures know the power of such a seal. You must come with me to see King Solomon."

"I will be no human being's slave!" Asmodeus bellowed.

His shouts shook the trees and rocks and caused Benaiahu to lose his balance and fall.

"You are no one's slave," explained Benaiahu respectfully, after he had stood up again and brushed himself off. "Solomon merely requests your services and then he will release you."

The giant demon had no choice so he reluctantly followed Solomon's faithful servant down the mountain and along the paths that led back to the palace.

Asmodeus was ushered into Solomon's throne room.

"You have conquered the world of men," said the Demon King. "Now do you wish to conquer the demon world as well?"

"No," said Solomon. "That is not what I wish. But I do need to know something from you, and that is the location of the shamir, the special worm Moses used long ago."

Asmodeus stood in silence.

"Only so that I can complete the construction of the Holy Temple. Nothing more," Solomon explained patiently.

"The worm is not in my keeping," Asmodeus finally said. "It belongs to the Prince of the Sea. He entrusted it to a woodpecker who has sworn an oath to watch the shamir carefully. This woodpecker carries the worm to desolate mountaintops where nothing grows. First the worm splits the rocks on the mountaintop. Then the bird plants seeds he has gathered from other places in the cracks so that little shrubs and bushes and trees may grow."

Following Asmodeus's direction, Benaiahu located the woodpecker's nest. He covered it with a piece of clear glass and hid himself close by.

Soon the woodpecker came, bringing food for its young. But when it tried to enter the nest, it was blocked by something it could not see. It pushed and pecked and squawked until it had no strength. The babies on the other side of the glass peeped frantically.

Out of desperation, the bird flew to the shamir's hidden place to bring it back to the nest. As soon as the woodpecker put the worm on the piece of glass, Benaiahu appeared next to the nest and grabbed the glass with the shamir on it.

Carrying his prize, Benaiahu quickly climbed down the tree. The woodpecker followed, attacking him on his face and hands and back. But Benaiahu did not drop the worm. He ran so fast that he soon left the exhausted bird behind.

Benaiahu brought the shamir to the king. Now Solomon's problem of building the Temple without iron tools was solved. He went to see Asmodeus.

"Benaiahu found the worm as you directed," said Solomon. "But before I release you there is one thing I must know. Why are you, a demon, considered more powerful than a human if you can be captured by one of us?"

"If you remove my chains and give me your ring, I will show you why."

Solomon unfastened Asmodeus's chains, curious to hear his explanation. He gave him the ring engraved with the name of God.

The demon stretched to his full height. One of his wings touched the earth while the other reached as far as heaven. He snatched up the surprised Solomon in his thin, clawlike fingers, and hurled him far away from the palace. Then Asmodeus changed his form and took Solomon's place as king.

He covered his clawlike feet with stockings, for that was one part of his form he could not alter, and flung the king's ring into the sea. In this way, he could be assured that Solomon would never again have the power to regain the throne or capture him.

* * *

Solomon was unconscious for a long time after his fall. When he awoke, he looked no more like a king than the town pauper. His clothes were torn and dirty, his body bruised and achy. He was without coins or goods.

No one believed him when he said he was the true King of Israel. Instead they laughed at him. He was forced to beg for his bread and wander through the land.

"I, Solomon, was king over Israel once," he lamented to anyone who would listen. "Perhaps I did accumulate too many riches, too much gold and silver, too many horses and wives for myself and am thus being punished now. But I was a good king nevertheless, wise and just and loved by my people. God have pity on me, Your servant."

At the end of three years of wandering, Solomon came to the city of Ammon. There he was hired as a cook in the royal household. The foods he prepared were ones he remembered from his own days as king, and were so delicious that he came to the attention of the King of Ammon.

The King promoted him to the position of chief cook.

This is how the King's daughter, Naamah, met Solomon. She watched him work whenever she passed by the kitchens. She admired his handsome features, his strong ways, and wise manner, and fell in love with him.

The King of Ammon was enraged when he learned of his daughter's love for his chief cook.

"I will kill you both," he threatened Naamah.

"I will still love him," said Naamah.

But the King of Ammon could not bear to kill his own daughter or her lover. So instead he banished them to the desert where they would surely die of starvation.

Solomon and Naamah wandered in the desert for days, drinking when they could, eating what they could, until they came to a city by the sea. They begged enough money to buy one fish.

When Naamah cut open the fish to prepare it for cooking, she found a ring inside the fish's belly.

"Solomon! Look!" she called.

At once, Solomon recognized the ring. It was his very own, engraved with the name of God, that he had given Asmodeus.

He placed the ring on his finger and said to Naamah, "We will make our way to Jerusalem. They must believe this beggar's story now. But first we will praise and thank God for this fish and what it has brought to us."

* * *

Meanwhile in Jerusalem, the rabbis began to think the King's behavior odd. Not once in three years had he called for his trusted advisor Benaiahu. He stayed away from his wives, always covered his feet with long stockings, and wrapped his body in a long cape.

So when Solomon and Naamah appeared at the palace, the rabbis thought they might listen to this beggar's story after all, this beggar who claimed to be King and had so claimed for these three years.

"You must show us proof of your tale," the rabbis said, for they still did not recognize this shabbily dressed, weary-eyed man as their king.

"I have proof," answered Solomon, and showed them the ring.

"But who is that in the throne room, in your shape and your likeness?" they asked.

"Come. I will show you," said Solomon.

He marched into the throne room, much to Asmodeus's surprise and chagrin, and stood before the demon. The rabbis placed themselves a few paces behind and over to the side.

"I wear the ring!" announced Solomon, lifting up his hand. Then with a sudden unexpected movement, he bent down, and pulled off one of Asmodeus's stockings.

The Demon King howled.

The rabbis gasped when they saw his claw feet.

In an instant Asmodeus dropped the cape, stretched his batlike wings so that they touched heaven and earth, and flew out of the palace.

Solomon, dressed in royal robes once again, gladly regained his throne and ruled Israel with Naaman as his Queen. He never saw the Demon King again.

Gittin 68a,b

Alexander's Lesson

Alexander the Great, King of Macedonia and many lands beyond, was not a bad king. He valued learning, and sought to educate himself about the customs of all the peoples of his mighty nation. He was one king who allowed the Jews to be Jews.

Alexander loved to travel.

"I wish to visit Africa," he told his advisors. "I have never been there, but I have heard of their wise rulers and mountains of gold and diamonds. I wish to test these rulers' judgments and see the treasure for myself."

"But Africa is beyond the Mountains of Darkness," the advisors warned. "You cannot go there."

"I have been to the Near East and to Asia," said Alexander. "And now I wish to go to Africa. Find me a way."

The advisors conferred for several weeks and finally presented Alexander with a map and a pearl that would shine a light in his path as he traveled through the Mountains of Darkness. They brought him donkeys that would be sure-footed in the dark.

"Take these as well," the advisors said, handing Alexander coils of rope.

"What need will I have of these?" he asked.

"Fix them along the side of the road as you travel through the mountains so that on your return you will be able to guide yourself by them. For once you are lost in those mountains, you will never find your way home."

Alexander thanked his advisors and followed their directions exactly. He made his way safely through the Mountains of Darkness into the land of Africa.

What he met there greatly surprised him, for he entered a land of all women. Their land was rich in forests and rivers, wildlife and crops.

The lawmakers of this land were indeed wise and had heard of Alexander and his mighty empire.

"You do not think of waging war on us, do you, mighty king?" the leader asked. "For if you defeat us, what honor will you gain?

And if we slay you, people will say you were killed by a nation of women."

Alexander considered her words and agreed to a peaceful visit.

"I have traveled far. Please bring me some bread," he said.

"Surely," she answered.

She brought Alexander a loaf of bread. This bread was not made of flour and water, but of gold!

"Do people in this land eat bread made of gold?" Alexander asked, puzzled.

"No," she answered. "But if it was really bread you wanted, why did you not stay in your own land? Had you not bread to eat there?"

Alexander pushed the golden bread away. "I did not come here to taste your bread, but to observe your laws. I have heard tales of the justice of this land."

"Then you may come with me to the place where our laws are decided."

Alexander followed the leader of the land into a large room filled with chairs, tables, and books.

He listened to the first case. It involved two men from a neighboring land who had traveled to the court in the hope of a fair decision.

"I bought land from this man a year ago for a fair price," said one. "While I was tearing down the ruin of a building that was on it, I found a chest of great value. Since I did not buy this chest, I tried to give it back to the seller. I pride myself on being an honest man. But he would not take the chest."

"It is not mine to take," said the seller of the land. "When I sold him the land, I sold him everything that was on it and in it as well. I too am an honest man."

The judge listened carefully to the men's stories. Then she said to the first, "Do you have a son?"

"Yes I have," he answered.

She turned to the seller. "And do you have a daughter?"

"Yes," he said.

"Then arrange for them to marry and in that way you will be able to share the treasure between you," said the judge.

As soon as she had spoken, the judge noticed that Alexander was laughing at her.

"Why do you find my decision amusing?" she asked.

"In my kingdom, we do not judge cases in this way," he

· *33* ·

explained. "In my kingdom, we would have ordered both men killed and taken the chest to the royal treasury."

The judge looked at Alexander very seriously.

"Does the sun shine in your kingdom?"

"Well, of course," answered Alexander, his smile fading just a little.

"And do you have cattle and sheep and goats in your kingdom?" she asked.

"Yes, of course we do," answered Alexander. "What does all this have to do with your judgment?"

"It is only for the sake of your animals that the sun shines in your land," she said. "Because the people are not deserving of it."

Alexander sat stunned. He neither spoke nor moved, but continued to listen to the cases in this court and the judges' wise and caring decisions.

And when he left this land to travel back through the Mountains of Darkness, he wrote on the city gates, "I, Alexander of Macedonia, was a fool until I came to this land of women in Africa and learned from their wise ways."

Tamid 32b

Never Too Poor to Study Torah

Hillel was one of the greatest of the Jewish sages at the time of the Second Temple. But as a young man, he was very poor and had to work hard to save enough money for study.

Each day he divided his earnings, half for his family and half for admission to the House of Study. One Friday during the winter, Hillel searched all day for work but could find none at all.

When he went to the study house, the guard would not let him enter without the customary fee. Hillel yearned to hear the words of the living God from his teachers, Shemaiah and Avtalyon, so he circled the building, hoping to hear them. But nowhere could he catch the sounds of teaching and the responses of the students.

Then Hillel spotted a skylight on the roof. He climbed a ladder by the side of the building and sat by the window, straining to hear every precious word that came through the cracks around the skylight.

So happy was Hillel to hear the teachings that he did not notice darkness approaching or snow beginning to fall. He listened, soaking in words of Torah even while the cold made him drowsy and sleepy.

After a while, Hillel could no longer pay attention and he fainted from the cold. Shemaiah and Avtalyon and their students welcomed the Sabbath. They prayed. They went home and ate the Sabbath meal. And they returned to study through the night. All the while, Hillel lay on the roof, half frozen under the snow.

At dawn, Shemaiah missed seeing the daylight filling the House of Study.

"Brother," he said to Avtalyon, "why is it becoming light outside, yet our house is still filled with darkness?"

Avtalyon glanced up.

"What!" he cried, and jumped to his feet. "That looks like a man's face on the skylight!"

Shemaiah and Avtalyon climbed quickly up the ladder and started scooping snow off the roof, off the person on the skylight.

Soon they discovered who the person was.

"It's our student Hillel!" said Shemaiah. "And his body is stiff with the cold."

Shemaiah and Avtalyon and several of their students struggled to bring Hillel down into the House of Study. They cared for him, very slowly bathing and rubbing his body and warming him by the fire. Even though it was the Sabbath, they could do all these things to save his life.

Slowly, slowly, Hillel revived. He moaned and opened his eyes, surprised to see his teachers and friends gathered around him.

"Such a man is Hillel," said Avtalyon, "that he would give up his life for the study of Torah."

Yoma 35b

A Test of
Hillel's Patience

O nce two friends were arguing about the famous teachers of Torah in Jerusalem, Hillel and Shammai.

"Shammai yells every day, but I have never seen Hillel lose his temper," said the first. "He speaks kindly and lovingly to everyone."

"I do not believe it," said the second. "There is not a person on earth who does not get angry sometimes."

"I will wager four hundred coins that no matter what you do, Hillel will remain patient with you."

The second man laughed. "An easy bet."

He waited until just before the Sabbath, a time when all Jews were very busy, and walked over to Hillel's house.

"Is Hillel here? Is Hillel here?" he called through the doorway.

Hillel was washing his hair in honor of the Sabbath, but he stopped and got dressed.

"Yes, my son? What do you need?" he asked politely.

"I have a question," said the man.

"Go ahead, ask," said Hillel.

"Why do Babylonians have round heads?"

"A good question," answered Hillel. "Perhaps you were not aware that I am from Babylonia myself. So I would know that the midwives there are not well trained in the proper way to hold a new baby's head."

"I see," said the man and left.

This Hillel is not like Shammai, he thought. Shammai would certainly have chased me out of his house with a measuring stick for bothering him with such a question before the Sabbath. He chuckled. But I have other questions.

He waited just long enough to allow Hillel to begin his preparations again. Then he walked to Hillel's door.

"Is Hillel here? Is Hillel here?" he called.

Hillel stopped washing his hair and dressed once again. "Yes, my son? What do you need?" he asked politely.

"I have a question," said the man.

"Go ahead, ask," answered Hillel.

"Why do Tadmorians have round eyes?"

"A good question," answered Hillel. "It is because they live in sandy places. If they had narrow eyes, the sand would always catch in the corners of their eyes and hurt them."

"I see," said the man and left.

This Hillel is a different sort, he thought. But there is no one on earth who does not get angry sometimes. He waited just long enough to allow Hillel to begin washing his hair again. Then the man walked to Hillel's door.

"Is Hillel here? Is Hillel here?" he called.

Hillel stopped washing and got dressed a third time.

"Yes, my son? What do you need?" he asked politely.

"I have a question," said the man.

"Go ahead, ask," said Hillel.

"Why do Phrygians have wide feet?"

"A good question," answered Hillel. "It is because they live in marshy places. Their wide feet help them walk where it is muddy."

This time, the man did not leave. He was determined to make Hillel lose his patience.

"I have many questions to ask," he said to Hillel, "but I am afraid you will become angry with me."

Hillel patted the cloth around his wet head and sat down beside the man. "Come. Ask all your questions."

The man could not believe what he was hearing. Here it was right before the Sabbath, the busiest time of the week, and Hillel was prepared to answer all his silly questions. How could anyone have such patience?

"Are you the Hillel who is called the Nasi, the head?" he asked angrily.

"Yes," Hillel answered.

"Then may there be no more like you!"

"But why, my son?" Hillel asked, still calm and polite. He knew he had tried his best to listen to this young man.

"It is because of you that I have lost 400 coins," the man complained. He told Hillel of his wager.

"It is better that you lose 400, even 800 coins," said Hillel, "than that I lose my patience."

Shabbat 30b–31a

· 37 ·

Learning Torah on One Foot

Two of the teachers in Jerusalem at the time of the Second Temple were Hillel and Shammai. Both were great scholars and both had many students, but Shammai was known for his strictness and Hillel for his patience.

Once a non-Jew came to see Shammai. "I do not have the time to study your laws, your Torah, every day like these students," he said, pointing to the crowded room, filled with books and students. "But I would like to become a Jew if you can teach me the whole Torah while I stand on one foot."

"What these men study their entire lives, you expect to learn in one minute?" Shammai replied in anger. "That is a ridiculous request. Get out of here." And Shammai pushed the man out with his measuring stick.

So the non-Jew went to see Hillel. "I do not have the time to study the laws every day like your students," he said. "But I would like to become a Jew if you can teach me the whole Torah while I stand on one foot."

Hillel did not shoo the man away. Instead he gave the request some thought and finally agreed.

Hillel waited while the man stood carefully on one foot and lifted the other.

"That which you hate, do not do to your neighbor," Hillel said to him. "That is the whole Torah. All the rest is explanation and commentary. Now learn the rest so you will truly understand what I have just taught you."

"I will," said the man. And he became one of Hillel's most devoted students.

Shabbat 31a

Honi the Circle Maker

This is how Honi came to be called Honi the Circle Maker.

It was the rainy season in the land of Israel, yet no rain fell. The people grew worried. With no rain, there would be no crops. With no crops, there would be no harvest. And with no harvest, there would be no food for either man or animal.

The people knew Honi to be a righteous man, a doer of good deeds who could pray to God with all his heart.

"Pray for us," they pleaded with Honi. "Pray for the rain we need."

So Honi prayed. He prayed with all his heart. But no rain fell.

Honi thought of the Prophet Habakuk, who made a circle and prayed from within the circle until God heard him.

So Honi drew a circle. He stood within it and said, "God, Your children have asked me to pray to You. I have something to ask of You as a child asks a parent. I pray for rain for Your thirsty earth and thirsty people. I will not move from this circle until You have mercy on Your children."

Honi looked at the sky. So did all the people. A small cloud formed. Then another. A light rain began to fall. Then it stopped.

"This rain will not save us or our animals or crops," cried someone near Honi. "God sent only enough rain so that Honi could move from his circle."

Honi heard and prayed even harder from his heart. "It is not this rain that we need, God, this trickle. We need rain to fill our pitchers and ditches, our wells and feeding troughs."

This time huge clouds formed and blackened the sky. The rains came down with great force, frightening the people.

"This rain will destroy the world," cried someone near Honi.

So Honi prayed a third time. "It is not for this that I have prayed, God, but for a rain that will bless the land and its people."

Then the force of the rains changed to a moderate flow from the heavens. The people happily set out basins and pitchers to catch the rain. They watched as their wells and ditches filled once again.

But the rains did not stop. The pitchers and ditches and wells

overflowed with water. Streets became like rivers with water streaming into homes and barns. The people grabbed what belongings they could and ran for shelter to the Temple, which stood on the high place in Jerusalem.

They sent a message to Honi. "You must pray yet again. Pray for the rains to stop."

"I have never before prayed that God stop a blessing. But I can see that there is now too much rain.

"Bring me an offering of thanks to God and I will do what you ask."

Honi placed his hands on the people's offering and prayed. "God, Your people cannot live with too much or too little, with too much blessing or too much trouble. May it be Your will to stop this rain so Your people can return to their homes once more."

As soon as Honi said these words, winds came and blew the clouds away. The sun shone and the people went thankfully back to their homes and fields, finding delicious mushrooms and truffles to gather from the moist earth beneath their feet and eat.

After thanking God with all his heart, Honi left his circle at last. The people remembered the miracle of the rains and called Honi by a new name in Israel, Honi the Circle Maker.

Ta'anit 23a

Honi and the Carob Tree

H oni, the miracle worker who lived during the days of the Second Temple, was on a journey when he saw an old man planting a tree.

"What kind of tree are you planting?" asked Honi curiously.

"A carob tree," answered the man.

"Doesn't the carob tree take a long time to bear fruit?" asked Honi.

"Seventy years."

"But you won't even be alive to eat the fruit of this tree," said Honi.

"No. But my grandchildren will be. Just as there were carob trees when I came into this world, so there will be carob trees for them."

Honi walked to a shady spot and sat down to eat his meal.

Such a long time and never to see the fruit, Honi thought. If he planted an olive tree or a fig tree, he might live to eat the olives and figs for his efforts.

With bread and drink filling his belly, Honi began to feel drowsy and soon fell asleep, as he often did in the middle of the day.

But Honi's sleep was not an ordinary sleep. For as he slept, the small rocks all about him slowly grew larger until they enclosed him and hid him from view. Nor was his sleep of ordinary length. For Honi slept not just one hour or two, not just one year or two or three, but for a full seventy years.

When Honi awoke from this sleep, he looked about in confusion. He did not remember these big rocks or the tall weeds.

How odd, he thought as he looked about. I will find the old man planting the carob tree and ask him why everything looks so different.

Honi followed a path through the boulders and saw the old man's field. There, where the old man had planted the sapling, was a tall, healthy carob tree with a wide trunk, glossy green leaves, and luscious pods of fruit. A young man picked the fruit and fed it to his little girl, who took great delight in sucking the sweet juices from the pulp.

Honi walked over to the young man. "I remember an old man planting a tree here," said Honi. "Do you know where I can find him?"

The man looked puzzled. "You couldn't be thinking of this tree," he said. "My grandfather planted this one seventy years ago. You must be thinking of a different tree."

"Seventy years ago!" exclaimed Honi. "Could it be that I have slept for so many years?"

He watched as the young man gathered the fruit in his baskets and the little girl ate from the pods, the juices trickling through her fingers.

How wise that old man was, thought Honi, to plant a tree not for himself, but for the generations to come.

It was then that Honi realized that his seventy-year sleep was a gift from heaven, a gift that made the old man's words as clear as the scene before him.

Ta'anit 23a

Nicanor's Doors

It was a joyous time in the land of Israel. The Second Temple was being rebuilt with new walls, columns, altars, and doors. The people helped in every way they could to make God's dwelling place beautiful.

Nicanor, an Alexandrian Jew, promised to donate to the Temple two magnificent doors made of the finest copper. He hired the best craftsmen in Alexandria to cast and decorate the doors and saw to it himself that the work was done properly.

Finally the day came when Nicanor gazed at the doors and knew they were ready to take their place in the Holy Temple. They shone from the many polishings. Their carvings were almost lifelike. Never before had such doors been crafted, and people came from all over the city to see them.

Nicanor himself went with the doors onto the ship that would carry them to Israel. He wrapped the doors in cloths and was determined to guard them on the entire journey to be sure they would arrive at the Temple unharmed.

The doors were so large and weighed so much that the ship had to sail slowly, and it took many more days than usual to reach Israel.

Late one afternoon, as sometimes happens at sea, a storm gathered. The sky grew dark with clouds, the winds blew stronger and stronger, and the waves tossed the ship carrying Nicanor and his gift.

As the storm got worse and worse, the sailors became fearful.

"We will sink," cried one.

"Look! The ship can't right herself," said another.

"The doors! They are weighing us down."

It was true. The ship was leaning to one side and water was pouring into it.

The desperate sailors took hold of one of the Temple doors.

"No! You must not," cried Nicanor, and he grabbed the sailor nearest him, trying to pull him from the door. But he could not stop the sailor, and in horror, Nicanor watched the great door drop into the sea.

The boat still rocked and leaned, and the waves pounded against its sides. Water drenched everything.

"It's not enough," cried a sailor. "We must throw the other door over, too."

The sailors all agreed and reached for the second door.

This time Nicanor jumped onto the door.

"No!" he called out. "If you throw the door overboard, then you must throw me over too!"

The sailors hesitated. And in that moment the sea quieted.

Nicanor sobbed from happiness. The door was safe. He could feel the solid wood under his fingers. But he sobbed from sadness too, for the door that was lying on the ocean floor would never stand in the most holy of places.

The days were calm as the ship sailed on to Israel. When they docked in the port city of Acre, Nicanor watched as the remaining door was carried onto land.

In his mind, he saw the door standing in the Temple by itself and he was filled with sadness.

"How can this be?" he moaned. "A door such as this on one side and nothing on the other."

Nicanor's thoughts were suddenly interrupted—whoosh! What was that sound?

Nicanor looked over toward the boat. Emerging from under the boat he saw the second door, still bundled, riding a wave toward the shore.

"It didn't sink!" shouted Nicanor joyously as he ran to where the door had washed ashore.

Had it been carried in the current behind the boat all the way to Israel? Or had it stuck to the boat's bottom somehow? Nicanor did not know. He would never know. But he and all the people of Israel rejoiced in the miracle of the doors' safe arrival. And they rejoiced to see the enormous doors standing in the Temple gate, glowing and unharmed.

Many years later, all the Temple's copper doors were replaced with gold ones. But Nicanor's doors remained untouched, a reminder of the miracle that had brought them there.

Yoma 38a

Rabbi Johanan's Escape

It was the days of the end of the Second Temple. Under the leadership of Vespasian, the Romans had surrounded Jerusalem and cut off supplies into the city.

The Zealots, a group of Jews who believed in fighting the Romans at all cost, had taken control of the city and were not allowing anyone to leave.

Within its walls, the people of Jerusalem were starving.

Rabbi Johanan ben Zakkai decided he must do something. He called for his nephew Abba Sikra, who was a leader of the Zealots, to come to him in secret.

"Look all around you, Nephew," said Rabbi Johanan. "The people are hungry. Many are already dying. How long will you Zealots continue this fight against the Romans?"

"We will fight until we all die, Uncle," said Abba Sikra. "Even though we have very little chance of surviving this siege, I cannot suggest peace. The other Zealots would kill me before they would surrender to the Romans."

"Then I must find a way to escape from Jerusalem and find help," said the Rabbi. "How do I get past your guards?"

"Not an easy task," said Abba Sikra. "No one has gotten past them."

Abba Sikra looked searchingly at his learned uncle, who was so kind and determined. He recognized the look on his face—the look he had when deciding the law in the case of a dispute. His eyes were focused and clear, his body tight like an arrow in a bow.

"The only people who have gotten past the guards have been the dead," Abba Sikra said, as if thinking out loud. "Carried in their coffins at great risk by family and friends to be buried outside the city."

"That's it!" said his uncle. "That's the way I will get out of the city. In a coffin! By pretending to be dead! I can trust my students Eliezer and Joshua to help me."

"I will help you in any way I can, Uncle," said Abba Sikra.

The next day, Rabbi Johanan remained in bed all day, suddenly very ill. Family, friends, and students came to see him with worried looks on their faces.

During the night, Rabbi Johanan motioned to the two students by his side.

"Our people here are starving and elsewhere they are being slaughtered by the Roman soldiers. I cannot sit by and see Judaism die. I must try to do something. It is time."

Though the two students were thin and pale from hunger and fear, they acted swiftly.

"We are lost!" they began to wail loudly. "Our teacher is dead."

Carefully and lovingly, they lifted Rabbi Johanan into the coffin and closed the lid.

"Can you hear us?" whispered Eliezer.

"Can you breathe in there?" asked Joshua.

"Yes," came the muffled voice of their teacher. "Don't worry about me. Just get me out of the city."

The two students lifted the heavy wooden coffin onto their shoulders and headed slowly for the closest city gate. As they walked down each street, up every alley, and around each corner, they searched the dark for Zealot guards. They saw no one until they came to the gate.

"Halt! Who goes there?" asked the guard.

"Our teacher died in the night." Eliezer spoke softly and evenly. "We want to bury him before the dawn."

The guard nodded. But then he lifted his arm high over his head, ready to drive his spear into the coffin.

"Wait!" shouted Joshua. "What are you doing?"

"Making sure only the dead pass this gate," the guard said, his spear still raised over his head.

"You musn't spear the dead body of our teacher," said Eliezer.

"Since when have Jews ever mutilated their dead? What a disgrace that would be before the Romans," said Joshua.

The guard hesitated. Finally he said, "You are right. Only Romans would do such things." He spat and jabbed his spear into the ground. "That's for the Romans."

He opened the gate just enough for the two students to pass with the coffin. "See that you return quickly," he warned. "The Romans . . . ."

Once outside the gate, Eliezer and Joshua did not speak as they searched for the shelter of some brush so they could put down their load.

"It's strange to be looking at Jerusalem's walls from the outside," whispered Eliezer.

"Yes. In hills full of Romans," muttered Joshua.

They listened and looked all around before lifting the coffin lid.

"Thank God," said Rabbi Johanan as he climbed out of the box. He breathed heavily of the night air. "Abba Sikra said it wouldn't be easy, but he never mentioned that the guards are accustomed to spearing coffins."

The Rabbi reached out for his students and embraced them warmly. Then he straightened up. "The Zealots are behind us and the Romans ahead of us."

Leading the way, Rabbi Johanan moved quietly through the brush in the direction of Vespasian's encampment. The three waited until dawn to give themselves up to the Roman guards, saying that they came to speak with the General.

"Peace to you, o King," said Rabbi Johanan when the guard brought him into Vespasian's tent.

"You have earned death on two counts, Rabbi," answered Vespasian impatiently. "First, I am not King, yet you call me King. Second, you say you seek peace, yet you have taken a long time to come to me."

"You will be called King soon," explained Rabbi Johanan, "since it is written that Jerusalem will fall to a king. And I could not come sooner because the Zealots among us would not let me."

"Make way," a guard interrupted Rabbi Johanan. "Here's a messenger from Rome."

A soldier, dusty from road travel, entered the tent.

"You are needed in Rome, sir. Immediately," he told Vespasian. "The Emperor is dead, and by the nobles of Rome, you are made Emperor." The soldier got on his knees on the floor of the tent and bowed before Vespasian.

The stunned general looked at Rabbi Johanan.

"Seeing that you are so wise, Rabbi, I will grant you a request before I leave and my son takes my place here. But do not be so foolish as to think I will stop the siege of Jerusalem."

A look of sorrow crossed Rabbi Johanan's face as he thought of the Temple that would now surely be destroyed, and of his friends, family, and students still in the city.

But he straightened up and faced Vespasian. "Then I ask that you promise safety for the city of Jabneh with all its sages, including the family of Rabban Gamaliel."

"Agreed," said Vespasian. He called to one of his officers. "See that these three men reach Jabneh safely," he ordered.

As the three sages left the camp and looked once more at the doomed city, Rabbi Johanan tried to comfort his students, though his own voice was heavy with sadness. "At least Judaism and the Torah will not die with the destruction of the Holy City but will live on in Jabneh."

In his determined way, Rabbi Johanan went on to establish Jabneh as the religious and national center of Israel, despite the ruin of its heart, Jerusalem.

Gittin 56a

The Argument

The two rabbis argued back and forth, back and forth, as they sat in the high court at Jabneh in the days after the destruction of the Second Temple.

Their discussion was about an oven. Rabbi Judah said that the oven was impure, not kosher, whereas Rabbi Eliezer, one of the most learned of the sages, was of the opinion that it was pure—kosher.

The rabbis argued for a long time, because no matter of law was trivial to them. Minor matters, major matters, all required serious attention.

The other sages of the high court listened and added their opinions. In the end all the sages except for Rabbi Eliezer agreed with Rabbi Judah.

"I know I am right," said Rabbi Eliezer, unwilling to give in to the majority. "I will prove it."

He stood up and pointed to the large tree in the courtyard.

"Do you see that carob tree?" he asked. "If the law is as I say, then that carob tree will prove it."

The sages all turned to look at the tree. While they watched, the tree uprooted itself, sailed through the air, and put down its roots 100 cubits away.

"Amazing!" said one sage.

"Unbelievable!" said another.

Then everyone was silent until Rabbi Judah turned to look squarely at Rabbi Eliezer.

"A carob tree cannot prove a law right or wrong," he said. "In this court, we do not decide laws in such a way."

Rabbi Eliezer, however, would not give up.

He pointed to the stream that ran outside the House of Study.

"If the law is as I say, then this stream will prove it."

The sages turned, a bit nervously, to look at the stream. They did not know what to expect.

What they saw was another miracle. The water stopped flowing in its normal direction, stood motionless for a time, and then reversed so that it ran the other way.

Fish leaped out of the water. Birds stopped singing. Rocks and pebbles were tossed onto the banks.

The sages were silent once again.

Then Rabbi Judah addressed the court.

"How can a stream's direction decide a law? We do not prove right or wrong in such a way."

This time Rabbi Eliezer pointed to the very walls of the House of Study.

"If the law is as I say, then these walls will prove me right."

As he spoke, the walls slowly moved, closing in on the sages while they sat in assembly. The room was filled with the grating and creaking sound of blocks of stone resettling.

Rabbi Judah scolded the walls saying, "Stop! Why do you interfere in a dispute among Torah scholars in this way?"

Immediately, the grating and creaking ceased. The walls neither moved forward onto the scholars nor back to their original positions. They remained in a leaning position out of respect for both sages, Rabbi Joshua and Rabbi Eliezer.

But Rabbi Eliezer was not one to give up so easily. He looked up and said, "If the law is as I say, then let it be proved from above."

In the silence that followed the sages sat and waited. Never had they witnessed a day such as this one in the court.

Just as the tree flew and the stream flowed backwards, just as the walls moved, there was a voice that filled the House of Study, yet belonged to no one in the room. The voice sounded as if it were coming from above and from below, from this side and that side all at once.

"In all matters, the law agrees with Rabbi Eliezer," said the voice.

The silence that followed was as awesome as the voice that had spoken.

Only Rabbi Judah dared to break the silence.

"Listen to me, God and my fellow sages. The Torah itself tells us that it is no longer in heaven, but was given to the people at Mount Sinai. It is our guide. In our study and discussion of its laws, we reach our decisions. That is how we are to govern ourselves."

"That's true," added Rabbi Reuven. "The Torah itself says we are to agree on our decisions by a majority. The law is in the hands of the court and not in the hands of one single person, even though that person may be the learned sage, Rabbi Eliezer."

The other rabbis began to talk too.

"Yes, that is true."

"What they say is so."

"One person cannot . . . ."

The murmuring among the scholars continued until Rabbi Judah spoke again. "With all respect to Rabbi Eliezer and the miracles we have seen today, we still uphold that our way to decide laws is by the majority opinion of this court."

All agreed, except for Rabbi Eliezer.

* * *

Years later, Rabbi Nathan, one of the rabbis present at the court on that day unlike any other, met an old man selling bowls and knives. He sensed that this peddler was no ordinary peddler. Why, he did not know.

Stopping to buy a kneading bowl for his wife, Rabbi Nathan drew the peddler into a conversation. He found him to be wise and full of knowledge.

"What may I call you, old one?" asked Rabbi Nathan as the peddler gathered his belongings at the end of their conversation.

"You may call me Elijah," said the old man.

"It is as I suspected," said Rabbi Nathan. "You *are* no ordinary peddler. Before you leave on your journey may I ask you one more question?"

"Yes," agreed the Prophet Elijah.

"That day—do you know of it? When the walls moved and the voice called out in the House of Study?" Rabbi Nathan asked.

Elijah nodded. "I remember," he said.

"I have always wondered what God thought of the argument and the court's decision. It was not an easy thing to disagree with Rabbi Eliezer."

Elijah smiled for the first time that Rabbi Nathan could remember in their long conversation.

"God was pleased," Elijah said, "to see that the scholars were not so frightened by the miracles that they would give up their responsibility to discuss and decide the laws together as a court.

"It was true that Rabbi Eliezer was right in his decision about the oven. But it is also true that the law is no longer made in heaven but on earth, so that people may learn and grow by it."

With that, Elijah put his last bowl in his sack, nodded at Rabbi Nathan, and set out on the road ahead of him. He left behind a Rabbi Nathan who smiled with satisfaction at the Prophet's answer.

Baba Metzia 59b

A Thief in the Night

One day a Roman passed by the house of Ima Shalom, Rabbi Eliezer's wife. The stranger teased her, saying, "Your God is nothing but a thief. For even in your own Torah it says that God caused a deep sleep to fall upon Adam. And while Adam slept, God took one of his ribs to form Eve."

Ima Shalom seemed to ignore what the Roman said. Instead, very distraught, she called for a guard.

"Why are you calling for a guard?" asked the Roman in surprise.

"Thieves visited us last night," she answered. "They took our silver pitcher and left a gold one in its place."

The Roman laughed. "I wish a thief like that would visit me every day, and leave me richer than I was before."

Ima Shalom smiled.

"Aha. That is exactly what happened to Adam," she replied. "God took a rib from him and gave him a valuable gift instead, a wife."

"But why did your God have to put Adam to sleep and act like a thief in the night?" continued the Roman, still not satisfied with what Ima Shalom said.

Much to the Roman's bewilderment, Ima Shalom did not answer him directly, but sent for a piece of raw meat.

Right before the Roman, she placed it under her arm. Then she took it out, roasted it, and offered him a piece to taste.

"I cannot eat that," said the Roman. "Not after I have seen what you have done with it."

"That is how Adam would have felt if God had allowed him to watch the creation of Eve from his rib," she answered.

The Roman shrugged his shoulders and left, knowing he had been outwitted.

Sanhedrin 39a

The Goats That Once Were Chickens

One hot afternoon, Jacob walked home carrying a sackful of chickens he had bought at the marketplace. He was tired, and when he saw the shady doorway of a house, he stopped to rest. Carefully he placed the chickens on the ground beside him, leaned back, and fell asleep.

"Sleeping, Jacob?" His friend Avram woke him up. "Come. Miriam sent to me look for you. Don't you know how late it is?"

Jacob was so flustered by his friend's message that he jumped up and went with Avram, leaving his chickens behind.

Cackle. Cackle. Cackle. The chickens' noises grew louder and louder as they squirmed in their sack, trying to free themselves.

Rabbi Hanina ben Dosa, who lived in the house, heard the noise. "Those chickens sound like they're in our yard," he said.

"I'll go see," said his wife.

When she stepped outside, she saw the wiggling sack tied with green rope near the doorway.

"What shall I do with this?" she asked her husband, showing him the sack.

"Probably the owner forgot them," Rabbi Hanina said. "We'll care for his chickens until he comes."

Rabbi Hanina's wife fed the chickens and gave them water. They ran around in the yard, and in and out of the house.

One day went by. Two. Three. More. Still the owner did not come for his chickens.

The hens began to lay eggs. The Rabbi's wife brought the first one to show her husband.

"Look, we have eggs now," she told him.

"We musn't eat any of the eggs," Rabbi Hanina said. "They belong to the owner. He'll come back for them."

Even though the Rabbi and his wife were very poor and sometimes hungry, they left the eggs alone. The hens sat on their eggs and before long, the eggs hatched into active little chicks.

Hen, roosters, and chicks filled the yard and the house, scrambling under tables and chairs while Rabbi Hanina studied and his wife cooked and baked. Cackle, cackle. Cock-a-doodle. Cheep, cheep. Sounds also filled the yard and the house.

Two months went by. Three. Four. More. Still the owner did not come for his chickens.

"We must do something," said the Rabbi's wife, as she scattered the last of the chickens' grain around the yard.

"Yes, we must," agreed the Rabbi, who had to study with his fingers stuffed in his ears. "I know. I'll sell the chickens and buy goats. We won't have to feed the goats. They can graze on the forest floor."

One year went by. Two. Three. More.

Then one day, Jacob was walking near Rabbi Hanina's house with Avram when he stopped.

"Avram," he said. "Remember that time I forgot my chickens? I went looking for them, but couldn't find the right house or the sack?"

"I remember."

"This house reminds me of the one I stopped at to rest."

Rabbi Hanina, who had been standing by the open window and heard Jacob, came running out of his house.

"Friend. Stop a minute. What kind of sack did you say you left?"

Jacob straightened suddenly, startled by the Rabbi.

"Why, years ago I left a large sack of chickens tied with green rope near here."

"Then I have something to show you." Rabbi Hanina led Jacob and Avram to the goat shed. "Here are your chickens. You may take them with you."

"But these are goats!" Jacob looked very confused.

Rabbi Hanina laughed.

"Your chicken family grew so large that I sold them and bought goats."

"Rabbi Hanina, you are so kind. I've never met anyone so careful to return lost things," said Jacob. He tied up the goats and led them out of the yard with Avram.

Jacob smiled and waved.

Rabbi Hanina ran inside to tell his wife.

"The owner came for his chickens," he called.

"At last. It was a good thing we kept them for him all these years," said his wife. "But tell me, did he recognize them?"

Ta'anit 25a

The Hallahs

It was almost the Sabbath. But in Rabbi Hanina ben Dosa's house, there was very little food for the festive meal. There were carobs from the carob tree growing in front of his house, but there was no meat or wine or braided breads—hallahs.

Rabbi Hanina was known as a doer of good deeds and his wife was as pious as her husband. She did not complain that they were poor and sometimes hungry. But she did worry that her neighbor, a prying gossip, would notice that there was no smoke coming from her chimney, no hallahs baking in the oven. Her face grew hotter and hotter, redder and redder as she thought of her neighbor laughing with the other women over how poor she was.

Then the Rabbi's wife smiled. I'll fool her by having a fire anyway, she thought. She walked over to the woodpile, picked up some sticks, and built a fire. Soon there was smoke coming from her chimney as well.

Before long, her neighbor noticed the smoke. "Ah, the rebbetzin is baking today for the Sabbath. But how can that be? Just yesterday, when I happened to be standing near their window, I heard her tell the Rabbi that she had no flour left. I'll go over, wish her a good Sabbath, and while I'm there, take a quick look to see what is indeed baking in her oven."

Rabbi Hanina's wife saw her neighbor walk toward her door.

"Oh, oh, trouble. She wants to see what I'm baking. Oh, God, is there anything I can do?"

Rabbi Hanina's wife ran and hid in the next room so she would not have to open the door.

Knock, knock.

The neighbor waited for an answer. There was none. She knocked again. Still no one came to the door. So she opened it herself.

She walked into the kitchen and over to the oven. To her surprise, loaves of browning hallahs filled the oven and on the table nearby, more loaves awaited their turn to be baked.

"Rebbetzin, Rebbetzin, come quick. Bring your bread shovel or your hallahs will burn!" the neighbor called.

"Coming!" Rabbi Hanina's wife ran into the kitchen, carrying her bread shovel.

She looked into her oven and saw the hallahs as surely as did her neighbor. Beautiful, big, round hallahs all twisted and shaped, ready for the Friday night meal.

Calmly, she shoveled the hallahs out of the oven and put the braided dough in their place to bake.

"Good Sabbath," she said to her neighbor. "Thank you for keeping an eye on my hallahs."

"Good Sabbath," replied the neighbor, who felt a little disappointed.

Rabbi Hanina's wife saw her out the door.

"Thank You," she whispered looking up. "We may be poor in some ways, but we are not poor in our love for God or in our experience of miracles."

Ta'anit 24b

A Banquet for God

The Roman Emperor Hadrian was very proud of the elaborate banquets and entertainments he hosted. After all, who else in the whole world could afford so much food and so many performers? Who else in the whole world was so powerful and had so many servants to do his bidding?

Hadrian's chest swelled with the thought of his might and power. Just one little thing bothered him. It was that last conversation he had with Rabbi Joshua ben Hananiah, whose God he could neither see nor touch.

There must be some way, he thought, that I can show Rabbi Joshua and his God just how powerful Hadrian, the Roman Emperor, is.

Hadrian paced up and down the throne room and then he smiled.

"Guard!" he called. "Go fetch Rabbi Joshua. Immediately! He's staying at David ben Amram's inn."

Rabbi Joshua hurried to the palace. Would the Emperor ask him another one of his questions? Or would he tell of another of his laws that would make things harder for the Jews?

Hadrian was waiting for Rabbi Joshua in the throne room. "Ah, Rabbi Joshua," he said. "There is something I would like to do for which I need your advice. You know I am famous for my banquets and entertainments. I would like to honor your God with a banquet!"

Rabbi Joshua was stunned. This he had not expected. "A nice idea, Emperor, but one cannot make a banquet for God."

"Why not?" Hadrian's smile turned into a scowl. "Aren't I wealthy enough? Powerful enough?"

"You are indeed rich and powerful. But God has so many servants. There is no way to gather them all together in one spot."

"I am the emperor and I will do it!" Hadrian answered.

Rabbi Joshua saw that he would not be able to dissuade Hadrian. So he said, "Since no hall or palace is big enough, go to the shores of the great river Rebitha, and make your banquet there."

Hadrian sent his porters and cooks, his carpenters and laborers, to the shores of the Rebitha. For six months his servants worked there making enormous banquet tables, sewing cloths, carrying dishes, and preparing foods. The Emperor went there often to check on their progress.

At summer's end, just when all was ready, a tempest rose up from the waters, blowing and howling. It scattered everything in its path and swept all of it into the river.

The Emperor would not let himself be discouraged. "What is a little wind against the Emperor of all these lands?" He pointed in front of him and behind him. "Lands that extend far beyond what one can see."

He ordered his servants to prepare yet another banquet. For

six months they hammered and sawed, gathered and cooked. The Emperor went there often to check on their progress.

At winter's end, just when all was ready, storm clouds moved in and covered the skies. A heavy rain plummeted down on the tables, the platters of food, and the goblets of wine. It washed everything into the river.

"What's the meaning of this?" Hadrian demanded of Rabbi Joshua. "I make a banquet for your God and the wind carries it away. I make a second banquet and the rain washes it away. Is your God trying to offend the great Emperor of Rome?"

"The wind and the rain are but the servants of God, sweeping and washing before the arrival of the heavenly guests," said Rabbi Joshua. "If God's servants are so powerful, imagine how much more so God must be!"

"I don't know about this God of yours," Hadrian muttered. But he did not order a third banquet.

Rabbi Joshua sighed. Would the Emperor ever learn that one cannot give a banquet for the God whose presence fills the entire universe?

Hullin 60a

To Look at God

A s he had done many times before, Rabbi Joshua ben Hananiah traveled to Rome to speak with the Emperor on behalf of the Jews. Hadrian's rules made life difficult for Rabbi Joshua's people, especially the rules that said they must worship the Roman gods.

In the past, Emperor Hadrian had always asked Rabbi Joshua difficult questions. But each time, Rabbi Joshua had an answer for him.

I wonder what he will ask me this time? thought the Rabbi as he neared the palace on this hot summer day.

The palace guards recognized Rabbi Joshua from his earlier visits and allowed him to enter.

As he walked to the throne room, he passed statues of the Roman gods. One was of a woman riding a lion, another was of a winged man with a snake coiled tightly around him. Some of the figures wore robes and some did not. The Rabbi stared straight ahead.

"Well, it's Rabbi Joshua come to talk," said the Emperor to his guest. His eyes twinkled mischievously and he smiled broadly and confidently. "I have a question for you."

Rabbi Joshua nodded in a humble manner, as was his custom.

The Emperor stood up and waved his arm toward the statues flanking his magnificent throne. "Our gods have faces, some beautiful, some terrifying. Why doesn't yours? I want you to show me the face of your God. I want to know what your God looks like."

"It says in the Torah that no one can see God and live," replied Rabbi Joshua.

"Nonsense. Who could believe in a God he cannot even see?"

Rabbi Joshua considered the Emperor's question carefully. He knew that if he made a mistake, Hadrian might make the laws worse or even take away the Jewish people's freedom entirely.

Finally, Rabbi Joshua said, "Come outside with me and I will show you my answer."

Emperor Hadrian followed Rabbi Joshua into the hot, bright palace courtyard. Rabbi Joshua faced the Emperor.

"You must look up, straight at the sun to discover our God," he said.

"But of course I cannot," the Emperor replied, a bit impatiently. "You know very well no one can look directly at the sun, especially at this time of year."

"If you cannot look at the sun's face, how do you expect to be able to look at the face of God?" asked Rabbi Joshua. "The sun is merely a servant of God and its brilliance is infinitely small compared with the brilliance of God's presence."

The Emperor had no answer to give Rabbi Joshua and so he dismissed him. The Rabbi returned to his homeland where he and his people continued to pray to the God one cannot see.

Hullin 59b

The Emperor's Daughter and the Wine Vessels

On one of his trips to the Roman palace to represent the Jews, Rabbi Joshua ben Hanania met the Emperor's daughter. The princess was a beauty and knew it well.

After the Emperor's advisor introduced them, the princess said, "I have heard of your wisdom, Rabbi, but I did not realize that such great wisdom could exist in such an ugly vessel."

Rabbi Joshua showed no surprise at the princess's remark. He had learned to live happily with his appearance. The princess obviously made too much of hers.

By way of an answer to the princess's remark, the Rabbi said, "In what kind of vessel does your father, the Emperor, store his fine wines?"

Not knowing what this had to do with Rabbi Joshua's ugliness, the princess answered quickly and haughtily, "Why in clay vessels, of course."

"Why would nobility such as you not use the finest, most beautiful vessels of gold and silver for your wines? Why does your father, the Emperor, use clay as the common people do?"

Immediately after talking to Rabbi Joshua, the princess ran to the wine cellar. There she saw the ordinary clay vessels that stored her father's wines.

She went to her father and demanded that the clay vessels be changed for gold and silver, as befits a royal family.

The wine stewards, puzzled though they were by the princess's request, exchanged the vessels as the Emperor ordered.

Now when the princess visited the wine cellar, she was pleased to see rows of gold and silver instead of clay.

"Good. The finest wines are in the finest vessels," she told the stewards.

Since they could not but agree with the princess, they remained silent.

Each day the steward drew the wine and served it to the Emperor and his guests to accompany their elaborate meals.

At first, the Emperor and his guests enjoyed their drink as much as they always had. But one day, the Emperor spat out his wine.

"Steward," he called. "What you have served me is sour. I demand an explanation!"

The steward bowed, horrified. "All the wine is sour, your Highness," he sputtered. "Because . . . because . . . we were ordered to exchange the clay vessels for those of gold and silver." He sobbed, afraid for his life. "Wine must never be stored in metals."

"You may go," said the Emperor. "But have the princess sent to me."

The princess came before her father, all primped and adorned in jewels and silks. She was not afraid of her father's anger.

"All the wine is sour," the Emperor told her. "Who is it that said you should do such a stupid thing as change the clay vessels for gold and silver ones?"

"Why, it was that ugly man, Rabbi Joshua," she answered. "And you thought he was so wise, father."

"Bring Rabbi Joshua to me," the Emperor told his advisor. "And I will see why he would say such a thing."

Rabbi Joshua came quickly, knowing well the Emperor's temper.

The Emperor wasted no words. "Why did you tell the princess to put my wine into gold and silver? Explain yourself!"

The Rabbi, who had not known what the trouble was, relaxed.

"Emperor, I did not think that the princess would actually have your wine poured into gold and silver containers. You see, when the princess met me, she expressed surprise to find wisdom in such an ugly vessel as I. By way of a lesson, I asked her in what kind of container does her father, the Emperor, store his fine wine?

"I was hoping she would see that just as wine is kept in ordinary clay vessels, so can wisdom be found in a person who is not beautiful on the outside, that the finest wines are not always found in the finest vessels."

The Emperor, embarrassed by what his daughter had done, quickly dismissed the Rabbi.

Nedarim 50b
Ta'anit 7a,b

The Rich Man's Son

Eleazar was the son of a rich man. When his father died, he inherited all his father's property, whole cities and boats by the thousands. Many people worked for him on farms and in shops.

But riches did not give Eleazar happiness. Only when he could sit with his books and study, or discuss the holy books with other students and sages, was he happy. And when he understood a passage of Talmud for the first time, or saw looks of interest on children's faces when he told them a story from Torah, then he felt truly joyous. Owning a thousand ships could not give him that kind of joy.

Sometimes he even found his riches annoying. Morning, noon, and night when he tried to study, he would be interrupted.

"The keeper of your accounts is here to speak with you, sir," said one servant.

"We need to hire another cook," said another. "One who does not use the kitchen money to fill his own pockets."

"The matchmaker has a perfect girl for you in Lydda," said yet a third. "A scholar's daughter, fair and gentle."

Each day that Eleazar saw to the needs of his estate, he grew more and more impatient.

Finally, he called for Eliahu, his father's servant and friend.

"As of today, I put my estate in your hands, Eliahu," he said. "I know you will look after it well."

"But . . . but . . . where will you go?" gasped the bewildered servant. "This is your home."

"Wherever they study Torah, that is my home," answered Eleazar.

He changed his clothes for Eliahu's so no one would think him a rich man, and took a large sack of flour from the kitchen for making his bread.

Leaving the estate with little else, he felt free for the first time.

He traveled from city to city, province to province, studying Torah in each House of Study. He learned from this scholar and from that one, and delved into the mysteries of the sages.

Through his study and learning, he became a rabbi himself, Rabbi Eleazar ben Harsom.

One day he happened to be traveling on a road not far from his own estate. Two of his servants noticed him, and realized that this poor man with a sack of flour on his back looked familiar. Thinking that he was a servant trying to leave the estate without permission, they stopped him. They never suspected that this was their master.

"Halt! Where do you think you are going?" one servant asked. "Have you permission to leave?"

"You are mistaken," Eleazar answered. "I am no servant, but a scholar and a teacher."

"No. We recognize you. You are one of our master's servants," they said, and they refused to let him go.

Rabbi Eleazar did not know what to do. If I tell them who I am, he thought, they will insist on bringing me back to see Eliahu. Perhaps he is even looking for me now to answer questions about money and cooks and wives. Eleazar shuddered.

"I will give you money to let me go," begged Eleazar. "You can pay your master for any services of mine he will lose."

Eleazar showed them all the money he had collected from teaching his students and performing his services.

Finally, the servants agreed to let him go.

So Rabbi Eleazar, the rich man's son, was able to continue living his life as he wished, traveling from one House of Study to another, learning and discussing, arguing and teaching, and telling stories all the rest of his days. Filled with a life of Torah, he did not miss the riches he had left behind.

Yoma 35b

Rachel and Akiva

Rachel was the daughter of the wealthy landlord Kalba Savua. Though he had planned a match for her with a well-to-do young scholar, Rachel fell in love with her father's shepherd, the poor Akiva.

Before she would marry him, however, she told him how

important it was to her that he study Torah and become a scholar. "Wealth is not as important to me as learning," she said.

Because of his love for Rachel, Akiva promised to do as she asked.

Though they kept their engagement a secret, Kalba Savua learned of it. He called for his daughter and was so angry with her that he shouted, "How could you do this? You promised yourself to a poor shepherd without my permission. If you marry Akiva, you must leave my house and never come back!"

Rachel cried when she left her father's house because she loved him and knew she would not see him again. Nevertheless, she left her riches behind to marry Akiva, and went to live with him in a small hut.

Instead of fine furniture and fancy food, she slept on straw and ate bread. They were poor and worked hard. Akiva chopped wood and gathered hay. Rachel cared for the family. She cooked and cleaned and sewed for others.

Despite their poverty, she encouraged Akiva to begin his studies, reminding him of his promise to her.

"You have a good mind, Akiva, and will do well as a scholar," she told him.

But Akiva felt ashamed. Here he was a grown man and he could not even read the first two letters of the alphabet, the alef and the bet. How would he ever be able to do what Rachel wished? He thought about his promise often and was discouraged.

One day, as Akiva was walking through a field, he noticed a well with a large boulder next to it. There was something unusual about the rock and Akiva went over to it to look at it more closely. Straight through the middle of the boulder was a hole.

"How did the hole come to be in this rock?" Akiva asked one of the shepherds standing by the well.

"Oh, that," the shepherd replied. "Can't you see? The hole was formed by the constant dripping of the water from the well."

Akiva immediately grew hopeful. If water, drop by drop, could make such a hole in a boulder as hard as this one, then couldn't the words of Torah, letter by letter, make their way into his heart and head?

When Akiva returned home, he told Rachel about the rock and about his desire to study. The next day he entered the classroom.

At first, because he knew so little, he had to study with the youngest children. This embarrassed Akiva. Here he was a grown man studying with 3- and 4-year-olds.

"Do not worry," Rachel said. "People may laugh at you today. And tomorrow too. But soon they will become accustomed to seeing you with the children and they will not laugh."

Akiva found comfort in Rachel's words.

He worked hard. Because of his devotion and quick mind, in time he mastered the alef-bet and all that the teacher in Jerusalem could teach him.

Rachel was very proud of her husband.

"Now you must travel to Lydda where you can study with the greatest sages, Rabbi Eliezer and Rabbi Joshua," she told him.

"That will mean I will be gone from you and the family for a long time," said Akiva.

"Many husbands go off to study," said Rachel. "If I were a man, this is what I would chose to do. Just think. When you come back, we will all be so proud of you. What a great teacher you will become."

With Rachel to encourage him, Akiva set off on his journey to Lydda. He studied there for many years until he became a teacher himself. He felt proud that he had fulfilled his promise to Rachel and her dream for him.

I can return to my family now, Akiva thought. I have done what Rachel asked of me.

Akiva journeyed back to Jerusalem with many of his students. But when he reached his house, he hesitated, for he heard an old man talking to Rachel inside.

"How long will you live like this in poverty?" the old man was saying. "Don't you grow tired of waiting for your husband? Go back to your father and beg his forgiveness."

"No," Rachel answered. "I do not feel as you do. If my husband were to return right now, I would tell him to go back to Lydda and study further."

When Akiva heard his wife's words, he turned around and went back to the academy to do as Rachel wished.

He became an even greater scholar, one of the wisest rabbis in all the land of Israel.

After more years of study, he journeyed once again to his home and to Rachel. Thousands upon thousands of students journeyed with him to continue studying with their teacher.

Rabbi Akiva's fame spread before him and when he reached Jerusalem, all the people gathered to pay their respects to the great rabbi from Lydda.

When Rachel saw her husband, she immediately ran to him,

flying through the crowd as if she had wings. Her heart swelled with pride and love for this poor shepherd who loved her and kept his promise to her. To see him surrounded by so many students!

But one of these very students sneered at her; another made fun of her shabby clothes.

"Who is this woman? To think she can throw herself at our teacher like this!" they said.

To their surprise, the Rabbi's face lit up when he saw this poor woman and he reached for her to stand by his side.

"This is my wife," he told the students. "It is to her that you and I owe all our learning of Torah, for she encouraged me when I did not know the difference between an alef and a bet."

Just then, the crowd drew apart to make a path for the rich landowner, Kalba Savua, to pass.

He had heard that a great sage had come from Lydda and he had something important to ask him. Kalba Savua was so unhappy and so desperate with grief that he did not recognize his old shepherd with a gray beard and wearing a scholar's robe. Nor did he notice his own daughter Rachel standing there.

He looked straight at the Rabbi and said, "For a long time now I have regretted a vow I made in anger to my own daughter. She promised herself to a poor, ignorant shepherd who knew not even one word of Torah. For that, I told her to leave my house and never come back. But now I am sorry. I ask you, Rabbi, to free me from my vow and allow me to take my daughter into my home once again."

"If you had known that your daughter's husband would someday be a scholar, would you have made such a vow?" asked the Rabbi.

"No," said Kalba Savua sincerely. "If Akiva had known even one law, one section of the Torah, I would not have said such a thing. But he did not even know an alef from a bet."

"In that case, you are free of your vow, for I am that poor shepherd Akiva who married your daughter Rachel. And it is because of her that I have become an honored scholar."

Kalba Savua stood speechless in front of the great rabbi. Then he began to cry tears of joy. Rachel went to him and kissed him, happy to be reunited with her father.

"You and your family are welcome in my house," her father said. "And my wealth is yours."

So it was that Rachel, Akiva, and their children went to live in Kalba Savua's house. Once again Rachel sat on elegant chairs and ate fancy foods. But more important to her than any of these fine things was her husband and the wisdom he had acquired from studying Torah.

Ketubot 62b
Nedarim 50a
Pesahim 49

The Candle, the Donkey, and the Rooster

R abbi Akiva went on many journeys—sometimes to collect money for the poor, sometimes to urge the Roman rulers to change their cruel decrees.

On one journey, he set out with a donkey packed with everything he needed. He took a blanket to sleep on, food to eat, and water to drink, and he also carried a candle so he could study Torah at night. He took a rooster to wake him so he could study early in the morning.

Rabbi Akiva led his donkey along the road all day until he reached a small town at evening. He was tired and wanted to find a place to sleep.

He knocked at the door of an inn.

"We're full," said the innkeeper gruffly.

Akiva moved on and knocked at the door of a large house with many courtyards.

"We never take lodgers," the servant said sharply.

Knock. Knock. No, no. Everywhere Rabbi Akiva went, he was refused.

Standing in the street, he patted his donkey and said to himself, "Everything God does is for the best. We'll make our bed in the field we passed before we came to this town."

And so he did. Rabbi Akiva lit his candle, fed the donkey and

the rooster, spread his blanket on the ground, and prepared to study.

He was lost in the study of the laws of Torah when suddenly with a whoosh!—the wind blew out his candle and he could no longer read the Hebrew letters that danced along the lines of the scroll. Akiva said the Shema prayer and bedded down in his blanket.

Rabbi Akiva was not yet asleep when he was disturbed by roaring and braying. He arose and found that a mountain lion had attacked his donkey and carried it away!

Though sad, Rabbi Akiva knew in his heart that this too was for the best. Isn't that what he had learned from his teacher, Rabbi Nahum of Gimzo, long ago?

Rabbi Akiva made certain the rooster was calm before he settled down in his blanket once again.

Squawk, squawk. The loud crowing woke Rabbi Akiva. Startled, he jumped up and ran over to the tree where he had tied up the rooster. The rooster was gone too. Not a mountain lion this time, but a weasel had crept into camp and stolen his rooster.

Never have I had a night like this on one of my journeys, thought Rabbi Akiva. But surely this too is for the best.

The rest of the night passed peacefully. When Rabbi Akiva awoke in the morning, he prayed and studied and packed his belongings on his back. When he neared the town, he knew something was not right. Doors were hanging open, barrels were overturned, and where there should have been the sounds of men, women, and children, of cows and chickens, there was silence.

Rabbi Akiva saw another traveler on the road. "Do you know what has happened here?" he asked.

"I heard that a band of thieves captured all the villagers and their animals in the night," said the traveler.

It was then that Rabbi Akiva realized how his life had been saved. For if the wind had not blown out his candle, the robbers would have seen him. If the lion and the weasel had not captured the donkey and the rooster, the robbers would have heard them braying and crowing. And if the townspeople had given him shelter, the robbers would have taken him captive too.

"So these things were all for the best," said Rabbi Akiva. And he gave thanks to God before continuing on his journey.

Berakhot 60b

Prove It

Someone knocked on the door of Rabbi Akiva's House of Study.

"Come in," said the great Rabbi, interrupting a discussion he was having with one of his students.

The person who entered was a stranger. He did not wear the traditional ritual fringes nor did he have the long beard and hair of the Jew. His hair was cut in the Roman style.

"I have a question to ask you," the stranger said.

Akiva nodded.

"Who created the world?" the stranger asked.

"God, the Holy One," answered Akiva.

"Prove it," said the stranger, smirking.

"Come back tomorrow," Akiva answered.

After the stranger left, Akiva resumed his teaching. When his students asked him what he would say to the stranger the next day, Akiva answered only, "You will see."

The man returned the next day and knocked on Akiva's door in the middle of the morning.

"Come in," said Akiva, greeting the stranger. "Today, I have a question for you. What is it that you are wearing?"

"Why, a robe," answered the stranger, a bit surprised that Akiva should be interested in his clothing.

"Who made it?"

"The weaver," answered the stranger. "Of course."

"Prove it," said Akiva.

"How ridiculous," the stranger blurted. "Can't you tell just by looking at the cloth and the design that this is the work of the weaver?"

"And can't you tell just by looking at the world, that it is the work of God, the Holy One?" said Akiva.

The stranger looked dumbfounded. And as he had nothing more to say to Akiva, he left the House of Study, with a frown on his face.

Akiva turned and explained to his students, "Just as a house

was obviously built by a builder, and a garment sewn by a tailor, so the world was obviously made by a Creator."

Temura, Bait HaMidrash 1:113–114

Like a Fish Out of Water

During Rabbi Akiva's lifetime, the Romans passed harsh laws forbidding the Jews to study and practice the Torah. Even though the penalty for doing so was death, Rabbi Akiva continued to gather people together and teach the ways of the Torah.

One day Pappus ben Judah saw Rabbi Akiva teaching and asked him, "Aren't you afraid of the Romans, Akiva?"

"I can answer you with a story," said the Rabbi.

"Once a hungry, sly fox was walking by a river. He saw swarms of fish swimming frantically from one place to another. The fox called to one of the fish, 'What are you running away from, fish?'

"'From the nets the fisherman are casting,' answered the fish.

"'Why don't you and your friends come up on land and be near me where you will be safe?' said the fox, who knew what a tasty dinner the fish would be.

"'What a foolish fox you are,' said the fish, 'if you think we would be safer on land where we will surely die, than here in the water, which is our home and which keeps us alive.'

"We are like the fish, Pappus," said Rabbi Akiva. "And our Torah is like their rivers and streams. It nourishes us and keeps us alive. How much more in danger we and all the people Israel would be without it."

With these words, Rabbi Akiva turned to his pupils and resumed his teaching of Torah.

Berakhot 61b

A Little Grain

The sage Rabbi Elazar Ish Bartosa had a great reputation for giving charity—tzedaka. People who collected for the poor ran away from him, knowing that he would give them all the money he had and be left with nothing for himself.

Since his daughter was soon to be married, Rabbi Elazar set out for market to buy the grain for the wedding meal. As soon as the tzedaka collectors saw Rabbi Elazar, they tried to hide, but it was too late. He had seen them and ran after them.

"Please," he called. "Tell me why you are collecting money."

"An orphaned boy and girl are about to be married and they do not have the money to make a wedding," the collectors answered.

"Orphans!" Rabbi Elazar said sympathetically. "They need this money more than my daughter, who still has her mother and father. Here! Take all the money I have and use it for their wedding."

Rabbi Elazar emptied his pockets and gave all but one small coin to the tzedaka collectors. He used the coin to buy a little grain.

When he returned home, he placed the grain in the storehouse and went to the House of Study.

Later, his wife asked their daughter, "What did your father buy for your wedding meal?"

"He said he bought a little bit of grain," she answered. "I will go and see how much there is."

Rabbi Elazar's daughter went to the granary and pushed against the door to open it. But to her surprise, the door would not budge. When she peeked inside, she saw that the door was blocked by bundles and bundles of grain piled to the top of the storehouse.

She hurried to the House of Study.

"Father!" she called. "Come see what your good friend, God, did for you."

When Rabbi Elazar tried to open the door to the storehouse, he was startled to find bulging sacks of grain leaning against the walls and door.

"This is surely holy food," he said, once he overcame his

· 69 ·

surprise. And true to his reputation, Rabbi Elazar also shared this grain with the poor.

Taanit 24a

Both Good and Evil

Rabban Shimon ben Gamliel was at one time the leader of the highest court in the land of Israel, the Sanhedrin. Though known mostly for his wise judgments, Rabban Shimon was also a great teacher.

His servant Tabbai knew this well, for on many occasions, a task or a question or an errand would turn into a lesson.

Once Rabban Shimon asked Tabbai to buy him some good food at the market.

When Tabbai reached the market, he looked from stall to stall. Perhaps I should get sweet figs or a fresh fish, Tabbai thought. Or maybe a jar of olives or some newly baked bread.

He finally settled on a piece of cow's tongue, something the Rabbi liked very much, but hadn't eaten in a long time.

He carried the tongue home.

"What have you bought?" asked the Rabbi.

"Something very good indeed," answered Tabbai. "Some tongue."

"Thank you," said the Rabbi. "Now go and buy some bad food at the market."

On his way to the market the second time, Tabbai thought about Rabban Shimon's strange request. Why would the Rabbi want him to buy bad food? What was bad food? Good food, bad food. "There must be a lesson in this," mumbled Tabbai.

As he walked along the market stalls, Tabbai passed by the fruits and the vegetables, the fish and the bread.

"Bad food," he kept repeating to himself. "I must buy bad food. Rotten dates perhaps? A stale fish? What sense is there in that?" Tabbai mumbled as he walked, his thoughts a jumble in his head.

Then he passed the butcher's stall and saw a cow's tongue, like the one he had just purchased for the Rabbi. Suddenly, Tabbai's thoughts came clear and he smiled. "Aha, so that is the lesson," he muttered.

Quickly Tabbai purchased another piece of tongue and brought it home.

"What have you bought?" asked the Rabbi.

"Something bad indeed," answered Tabbai. "Some tongue."

"When I asked you to buy good food, you purchased cow's tongue," said Rabban Shimon. "And when I asked you to buy bad food, you also bought tongue. What is the meaning of this?"

"Good can come from tongue, but bad can also," said Tabbai. "When people use their tongue for study and prayer and for praises and kind words, they use it for good reasons. But when people use their tongue for slander and unkind words, they use it for bad purposes. Isn't this so, Rabbi?"

Rabban Shimon smiled at his servant. "You have fulfilled my requests perfectly, Tabbai. You have found something that can be both good or bad, depending on how we choose to use it."

Midrash Rabbah Leviticus 33:1

My Brother Ki Tov

Once there was a wicked innkeeper who lived in the south of the land of Israel. He would wake his guests in the dark of night to tell them that a caravan of people and animals was passing, headed in the direction they were traveling.

"Hurry. Join the caravan," he would say. "It's much safer to travel these woods with others than alone."

The guests would believe him, and as soon as they went out into the night, robbers would fall upon them and take everything they carried. The robbers would then return to the inn to share the stolen goods with the innkeeper, who had planned the whole robbery.

One night Rabbi Meir was a guest at this inn. Just as he always did, the innkeeper arose in the dark of night to wake up Rabbi Meir.

"Hurry. A caravan is passing. It is much safer to travel with them than it is to travel alone."

"But it is night," said Rabbi Meir. "And I must wait for my brother."

"You are much better off going now," said the innkeeper. "Tell me your brother's name and where he is and I will call him for you."

"He is in the synagogue and his name is Ki Tov," said Rabbi Meir, who then went back to sleep.

The innkeeper stood at the door of the synagogue and called Ki Tov over and over again, but no one came. Finally, when he went back to his inn, it was dawn and he found Rabbi Meir loading his donkey with his baggage.

"But, but, where is your brother?" asked the tired, disgruntled innkeeper. "I called all night for him at the door to the synagogue and no one answered."

"He is here now," said Rabbi Meir, "my brother, the morning. In the Torah, God calls the light ki tov, which means it is good. I do not travel without my brother, the light."

"But you said your brother was in the synagogue," answered the innkeeper, his voice choked with anger.

"One always finds light in the synagogue, even at night," said Rabbi Meir. "For the Torah is there, and it is the light that guides our way."

There was nothing the innkeeper could do, for he and his band could not rob Rabbi Meir in the daylight. In great frustration he stood and watched as the Rabbi and his donkey walked away from the inn, farther and farther down the road, completely undisturbed.

Midrash Rabbah Genesis 92:6

Better a Change Than Death

Rabbi Meir was returning home from a trip to a nearby city. He dreaded traveling on the road near his home, but he could not avoid returning to his house any longer.

He neared home in the middle of the afternoon, which was usually a safer time to travel than at night or early in the morning.

Looking about him warily, he observed every boulder and tree he passed, half expecting a robber to jump out at him and demand money.

He had heard that a few days before, robbers had attacked an elderly man carrying only a few coins. They were even known to steal from women traveling with small children.

Just as Rabbi Meir spotted the houses on the outskirts of his town, he felt the presence of someone nearby, someone staring at him.

Quickly he turned around and surprised the two tall, bony thieves who had been ready to jump him.

"How dare you attack a rabbi!" shouted Rabbi Meir.

"We don't care who you are," said one thief. "We just want your money."

The other thief grabbed Rabbi Meir by the hair and searched him.

"No money," he said. "Should I throw him into the ditch like I did with the old man?"

"No. Let him go. He's not worth our trouble," answered the first thief.

They pushed Rabbi Meir to the ground and ran off.

When the Rabbi reached his home, he decided to ask for God's help with the thieves. A passage from the Book of Psalms came to his mind: "May sinners disappear from the earth and the wicked be no more."

So he prayed, "Dear God, may it be Your will that thieves, such as the ones I met on the road today, all disappear from our earth and cease to do their evil deeds."

His wife, Beruriah, was standing nearby and overheard his prayer. She was a respected teacher in the academy. Even in her own time, her wisdom and sharp mind had made her a legend among scholars.

"Meir," she said when he finished, "I do not believe a prayer such as yours is permitted."

"No? But it says right in Psalms that sinners should—"

"Yes, I know the passage," Beruriah interrupted. "And it is true that thieves are sinners. But if they stopped stealing, they would no longer be thieves. Or sinners.

"So please, you do not need to pray for their deaths, evil though their deeds be. Pray instead that they stop stealing and change their ways. Then all sinners will disappear from the earth,

· *73* ·

as the Psalms say. They will disappear, but not die; they will change for the good."

Rabbi Meir looked thoughtful. Soon he smiled and nodded at Beruriah.

"As always your wisdom astounds me. You are right. It is better to pray for a person to change than for a person to die."

He turned, and deep in prayer once again, he chanted, "Dear God, may it be Your will that the thieves stop their stealing and repent of their evil ways. In this way, may sinners disappear from the earth."

The Talmud tells us that this prayer of Rabbi Meir's was answered. He was able to travel again without fear because the thieves repented and changed for good.

Berakhot 10a

Rabbi Shimon, the Cave, and the Carob Tree

One day, Shimon bar Yohai sat with two friends, Judah and Yosi. Another man nearby listened to the three rabbis talk. As Rabbi Judah looked out over the city, he said, "The Romans have not been all bad. They are great builders. Why, look at the new markets, bathhouses, and fine bridges they've constructed."

Rabbi Yosi was silent, afraid to say what he really thought about the Romans.

But Rabbi Shimon fiercely hated the Romans and their laws prohibiting Jewish customs. They had killed many Jews, including his beloved teacher, Rabbi Akiva.

"Whatever the Romans do is for their own good, not ours," he said. "The markets and bridges bring them profits and the bathhouses bring them pleasure."

This was not a good time to speak against Rome anywhere or to anyone. Yet the man who had been listening did not guard his tongue, but told others what the rabbis had said. The news of their conversation went from one person to another until it reached the Roman officials and eventually the emperor, Hadrian.

Hadrian was enraged. "This Rabbi Judah who praises us will be rewarded. Yosi will be sent to live in the distant city of Tzipori for his silence. And this Rabbi Shimon must die."

When Rabbi Shimon heard this, he said to his wife and son, "It is not safe for me here any longer. Come to the House of Study with me, Elazar. We will hide among the scholars and books, and study."

Each day Rabbi Shimon's wife visited her husband and son at the House of Study. Making her way secretly through the city streets, she brought them food and drink and news.

One day, she looked especially agitated on her arrival. "I heard that the Romans are sending more soldiers to find you," she told them. "Hadrian has not forgotten. I am afraid for your safety."

"You are right," said Rabbi Shimon. "I will have to leave the city. Elazar, will you come with me? We can continue to learn and study together in the caves near the town of Peki'in. Hadrian's soldiers do not even know they exist."

Elazar agreed. Rabbi Shimon's wife was relieved that her husband would not go alone.

As darkness fell that night, Rabbi Shimon and Elazar crept out of the city, not knowing when they would see their family and friends again. They made their way to the hills of Peki'in and looked for a cave that could be their home until the Romans gave up their search for them.

Some of the caves were so wet they could not live in them. Some were too small and cramped, or so large that they feared foxes and bears also call them home. They finally settled on a small cave that was dry and secluded.

"This one is perfect for us," said Rabbi Shimon.

"But Father," said Elazar looking about him. "What will we eat when the food Mama gave us is gone? What will we drink?"

"It will be easier to think in the morning," replied his father, "after we have slept."

It was true. They were both very tired. They piled brush on the sandy cave floor for beds and slept soundly through the dark night.

When they awoke, they could see the inside of their new home by the slim shaft of light that came through the cave opening.

Elazar stared thoughtfully at the light and the opening and then sat straight up. "What's that in the corner by the entrance?" he

said, excited and hopeful at the same time. "Why, Father, it almost looks like a tree."

"It is a tree," agreed Rabbi Shimon. "I'm sure it wasn't there last night."

The Rabbi went over and touched the tree. "It is real, sure enough," he said. "And it is a carob tree. Here is our food, Elazar. God has provided for us."

It was then that father and son heard a trickling sound coming from near the tree. Had it been there before, they wondered? Or had it suddenly appeared? As they approached the sound, they could see a natural well in the ground next to the carob tree.

"Before we eat and drink, we will thank God for our food and water," said Rabbi Shimon. And so they did.

After breakfast, they studied together. Because he knew the entire Torah and Mishnah by heart, Rabbi Shimon was able to teach it to Elazar. So every day they learned and discussed the sacred writings, listening to each other's interpretations of the words and growing in wisdom. Rabbi Shimon was well pleased with his son's interest and capacity to question and understand, and the two were not only father and son, but partners in study and learning.

As the days went by, Rabbi Shimon grew concerned about their clothing. "We do not know how long we shall be here," he told Elazar. "And our clothes are already frayed and torn."

So he devised a plan wherein they wore their clothing only for prayer. When they studied, they buried themselves deep in the sand and piled their clothes neatly in a corner of the cave.

The years passed. Rabbi Shimon and Elazar saw no one. They slept and ate, prayed and studied, and the light of the Torah filled the little cave with warmth and truth.

One day, while they were studying—their bodies buried in the sand—they were startled to see a figure approaching. It was the first person they had seen in twelve years.

The Romans have discovered our hiding place after all these years, thought Rabbi Shimon, as he and Elazar tried to burrow deeper in the sand.

But the man was not a Roman. He was old, and wore the clothes and beard of a Jew.

"Shalom," said the old man. "I come with news for you, Rabbi Shimon bar Yohai."

Hearing his name from a stranger's mouth amazed Rabbi Shimon.

"How do you know me?"

"I know," said the old man. "I also know that the Emperor is dead and his decree against you is annulled."

Rabbi Shimon looked quizzically at the old man. He seemed familiar, yet a stranger.

"Can we leave the cave, then, and journey home safely?" asked the Rabbi.

"Yes," answered the old man. "Just be careful when you enter your world again. You have been away from it a long time."

As Rabbi Shimon and Elazar eagerly brushed sand off their bodies and put on their clothes, Rabbi Shimon asked, "But who are you? What is your name, old man?"

"You know me well enough," the man answered as he turned around and disappeared through the hills.

"Do you know who he is, Father?" asked his son.

"Yes, I do," Rabbi Shimon said, his eyes sparkling with a smile. "There is only one person he can be, and that is the Prophet Elijah."

Rabbi Shimon and Elazar packed some carob pods and water and left their cave-home. They were much changed from when they first entered it, having been enriched by their years of learning and their growing love of Torah.

They also looked at the world differently.

When they came across a group of men ploughing fields and chatting about future crops, they could think of nothing but how these people were wasting precious study time.

"These men are free and all they do is talk about their work," complained Rabbi Shimon. "They could be engaged in learning. And we suffered for twelve years to be able to study Torah."

Because of Rabbi Shimon's and Elazar's intense years of sacred study, their levels of holiness had reached great heights. As Rabbi Shimon stared in disapproval at the field, the plants began to catch fire and burn.

Startled farmers ran in all directions, uncertain how the blaze had begun. There was no lightning, no source of fire.

A voice called down from the heavens. "Rabbi Shimon! Have you left the cave to destroy My world? You must return to the cave with Elazar to prepare for life with people."

So Rabbi Shimon and his son Elazar lived another year in their cave. They came to realize that people study Torah so they can live in God's world and apply its teachings to their lives with other people, as well as with God.

God called to them again. "Leave your cave now and see My world with new eyes."

This time Rabbi Shimon and Elazar left the cave just before the Sabbath. The first person they met was a man carrying two bundles of sweet-smelling myrtle leaves.

"What are those for?" asked Rabbi Shimon.

"I'm bringing them home to add a sweet smell to my house in honor of the Sabbath," the man answered.

Rabbi Shimon looked at his son. "See how the Torah and its commandments are still precious to our people? I think we are ready now to live among the people, to teach what we have studied all these years in the cave and to learn from others as well."

Shabbat 33b

A Wife's Love

Many years ago, a couple lived in the town of Sidon. They were married for ten years, but had never been able to have any children.

The husband desperately wanted children, and though he still loved his wife, he decided to divorce her in order to have children with another woman. This custom was not uncommon in those times and in those places.

The man and woman came before Rabbi Simeon bar Yohai to request a divorce.

"We still love each other," said the husband, "but we must be parted. In ten years of marriage, my wife has not borne a child."

"Then I suggest you make a great feast," said the Rabbi. "For just as you were married and began your lives together with festivity, so you should part with food and drink, and with relatives and friends."

The couple did as the Rabbi said. They made a great feast. They ate and drank. And the husband felt especially warm toward his wife.

"I wish to give you a parting gift," he said. "Pick out anything you want from my house and take it with you when you go back to your father's house."

The wife looked at her husband sadly, but agreed.

After the party, the husband fell asleep from so much food and drink. His wife called for the servants. "Lift my husband up and carry him to my father's house."

Later that night, when the husband awoke from his sleep, he called out, "Where am I?"

His wife ran over to the bed. "You are in my father's house."

"But what am I doing here?" her husband asked.

"Remember last night? You said I could take anything I wanted from your house and bring it here. There is nothing in the world I care for more than you."

Tears filled the husband's eyes and he leaned over and kissed his wife.

"Perhaps we should visit the Rabbi again."

"We did as you suggested," the husband said when he stood before Rabbi Simeon bar Yohai. "But we learned that we love each other too much to separate."

"Then stay together," said the Rabbi. "I will pray for you that your wife may bear a child."

The Rabbi prayed. So did the man and his wife.

Within a year, their prayers were answered and their lives were filled with the joy that a child brings.

Midrash Rabbah Song of Songs 1:4

Elisha and the Dove

In the times when the Romans ruled over Israel, there was a custom among the righteous to wear their prayer boxes, their tefillin, all day long. One box lay against their forehead and one on their arm. Inside these boxes were prayers that reminded the tzaddikim, the righteous ones, at all times of the presence of God and of the commandments.

As happened in those times, the Roman government passed harsher and harsher laws against the Jews. Wearing tefillin became punishable by death. Soldiers in the streets and marketplaces kept watch to enforce these laws.

Many Jews stopped wearing their tefillin in public, but put them on secretly at home.

One tzaddik, Elisha, was especially disturbed by this law. Wearing tefillin was so important to him, such a part of his life, that he couldn't imagine not doing so. He decided to wear his tefillin despite the law, wherever he was—in his house, in the synagogue, even in the streets—just as he had always done.

When he walked outside, Elisha tried to be careful and avoid the soldiers. But this was difficult, because there were so many soldiers and they were everywhere.

One morning as Elisha stepped out of the synagogue, a Roman soldier spotted him wearing his prayer boxes.

"You there! Stop!" shouted the soldier.

Immediately, Elisha began running toward his house. I must hide the tefillin, he thought.

He tried to outrun the soldier. But he could hear the soldier's sandals slapping on the street behind him as he drew closer.

Elisha ran faster. So did the soldier.

He's going to catch up to me, Elisha thought. I must do something.

So Elisha took off the prayerboxes as he ran and closed his hands around them.

"As its wings protect the dove, may You and Your commandments protect me," Elisha prayed.

The soldier caught up to Elisha and grabbed his arm.

Elisha stopped running and clutched his prayerboxes to him.

"I saw you wearing those leather boxes. Where are they?" demanded the soldier.

When Elisha didn't answer, he said, "What's that in your hands?"

"The wings of a dove," Elisha answered, thinking of his prayer.

"Then open your hands so that I may see," ordered the soldier.

Elisha opened his hands and there, in his palm, sat a strong white dove with its wings flapping against his fingers.

The soldier stared in surprise. Elisha's whole being filled with relief and joy, and with shaking hands, he held the bird lovingly, as lovingly as if it were his tefillin.

From that day on he came to be called by a new name in Israel—Elisha of the Wings.

Shabbat 49a

· 80 ·

Rabbi Hama's Son

Like other scholars of his time, Rabbi Hama bar Bisa left his hometown to study Torah in a faraway city. He was gone for a long time. Rabbi Hama benefited greatly by studying with some of the finest teachers of his generation, for he grew in both knowledge and wisdom. He would often think of his family, though, his devoted wife and children.

How were they? Did they have enough to eat? Were the children keeping up with their studies? How he wished he could teach them himself.

Then he would think how fortunate he was to have a wife who insisted that he study and become a great scholar. How willing she was to work hard and take care of the family. He could still hear her words of encouragement when he left.

"You have learned as much as you can in our small town, my husband," she had said. "Now you must go to the great academies. Study well and return to us a scholar and a teacher."

Rabbi Hama sighed and went back to his studies.

After some time, when he had learned the arguments of the rabbis by heart and could give judgments himself, Rabbi Hama journeyed back to his home.

As he walked down the street toward his own house, he noticed that the houses looked older and smaller than he remembered, but all the same, he recognized the town. Suddenly the Rabbi stopped. He recalled how Rabbi Chananya's wife had been so startled to see her husband upon his return from a long absence that she fainted and had to be revived.

Perhaps I should go to the House of Study first and send word that I will be home soon, he thought. That way my family can be prepared to greet me.

So even though he longed to see his wife and children, he turned away and went to the House of Study where he sent word to his wife that he would soon be home.

In the House of Study he saw several men, young and old, seated at long tables, studying and discussing Torah. Rabbi Hama joined them.

The young man sitting next to him began asking him questions and soon they were involved in lengthy discussions about the texts. Rabbi Hama was very impressed by the level of this young man's learning, but he was also sad.

If I had been home all these years, he thought, I could have trained my own children to be as learned as this fine student.

To the young man he said, "It is time for me to return home. I have enjoyed our discussions. Please let us continue them at another time." And Rabbi Hama left the House of Study.

Upon entering his house, he saw that it was not very different than it had been when he left. In the center of the room were the wooden chairs and the table, and against the walls were the beds and cupboards. But oh how different his wife and children were! Though his wife had lost her youthfulness, she was still beautiful to him. And his children were no longer babies, but tall and grown up.

"Oh, my Rachel and my Shimon!" Rabbi Hama hugged each child closely. He looked up at his wife. "And where is Ushya, our oldest?"

"Ushya was not here when we received your message," his wife explained. "But he will be home soon. Here, come eat what I have prepared for you."

Rabbi Hama sat down with his family and ate his wife's good bread and soup. He told her of all he had learned, and she told him how she had managed in his absence.

While they were in the middle of their meal, a young man entered the room. It was the same young student from the House of Study.

He must have found out where I live so he could ask me more questions, thought Rabbi Hama.

He stood up as a sign of respect for the young man's learning.

"Since when does a father rise for a son?" asked his wife, chuckling. "Are the customs so different where you have been?"

Rabbi Hama looked at his wife in surprise. Then he realized that this young scholar whom he so admired was his very own son Ushya.

Joyfully he hugged Ushya and said, "My father, Rabbi Bisa, was a scholar. I am a scholar. And now I see that my son Ushya is also a scholar!"

From then on Rabbi Hama was no longer sad about having left his son, and he enjoyed many Torah discussions with the fine young scholar Ushya.

Ketubot 62b

Judah and Antoninus

When Rabbi Shimon's son Judah was born, the Rabbi had to make a difficult decision. Would he circumcise his son? Jews had always done so, for it was a commandment from God. But Hadrian, the Roman emperor who ruled the land of Israel, passed a law forbidding circumcision. Anyone found cutting off the foreskin of a baby boy would be punished with death.

"We cannot go against the law of Israel," Rabbi Shimon said to his wife. "We must circumcise our son. Do you agree?"

His wife looked sadly at her baby, fearing for his life, but she agreed. She wished to keep God's commandments.

When his baby was 8 days old, Rabbi Shimon circumcised him.

When the Roman governor found out, he sent for Rabbi Shimon and his son. After examining the baby and discovering that the story about the circumcision was true, the governor looked up at Rabbi Shimon.

"You are a great leader of the Jewish people, Rabbi Shimon, head of the High Court. But you have disobeyed the law. I will let the Emperor decide on your case. Send the baby and his mother to Rome to stand before Hadrian. I will do as he commands."

Rabbi Shimon said good-bye to his wife and baby son, and prayed for their safety.

It was a long way to Rome, and mother and son traveled for days. Many times, the mother cried during the journey, tears for her baby, herself, and her husband. There would be no escaping the Emperor's demands.

One evening, when they stopped at an inn, they were greeted by the innkeeper's wife with more warmth than usual. She had also given birth to a baby boy who was the same age as baby Judah. Even though she was a Roman, the innkeeper's wife had much sympathy for Judah's mother.

"Why do you travel so soon after giving birth?" she asked.

"We are Jews," answered Rabbi Shimon's wife. "And we have circumcised our son, which is against the Roman law. I have been

ordered to appear before the Emperor." Tears rolled down her cheeks as she talked.

The innkeeper's wife listened quietly to her guest's story. She did not speak for a few minutes afterwards. Then she took Rabbi Shimon's wife's hand in her own.

"Take my son Antoninus with you to see the Emperor. He is not circumcised. Leave your baby here with me and I will care for him as if he were my own son. When the Emperor sees that the baby you carry is not circumcised, you will be free to return here and take your own baby home."

Her guest's face glowed with hope.

"I am so grateful. I will do as you say and care for your baby with all my heart."

The next morning, Rabbi Shimon's wife left the inn with baby Antoninus. She carried him as tenderly as she had carried her own son, and set off for Rome, this time with a more joyful heart.

When she arrived at the Emperor's palace, he was expecting her. He had received the governor's report.

As he unwrapped the baby, he said sternly, "You know this act means death for you and your family."

Rabbi Shimon's wife, shaking before the Emperor, did not say a word.

When the Emperor saw the baby's bare body, he looked up, puzzled.

"Why, this baby is not even circumcised."

He called for his advisors.

They looked at the little baby boy before them.

"This God of Israel is a strong God," said one, "and performs many wonders for those who follow the Torah. It is a miracle that has made this baby whole again."

Hadrian gave the baby back to his mother.

"What use is it for me to pass a law like this one if the God of Israel can do such things?" So Hadrian repealed his law against circumcision, and freed the mother and baby.

Rabbi Shimon's wife took baby Antoninus and traveled back to the inn. The innkeeper's wife met her at the door, her eyes filled with relief and gladness.

"Your plan worked," Rabbi Shimon's wife told her. "Thank you for lending me your precious one." She handed Antoninus back to his mother.

"And here is your Judah," said the innkeeper's wife, "a fine boy. May our sons always be friends and help each other in need as I have helped you."

And so it was. When Judah grew up, he became head of the High Court after his father. And when Antoninus grew up he became Emperor of Rome. The two remained friends, visiting each other, exchanging gifts, advice, and letters. And while Antoninus was Emperor, the Jews were permitted to observe all their laws without fear of punishment.

Menorat Hama'or
Tosafot to *Arodah Zarah* 10b

The Missing Ingredient

Unlike some of the Roman emperors before him, Antoninus respected the Jewish religion and was a friend to Rabbi Judah ha-Nasi. He often visited the Rabbi and enjoyed their discussions together.

Some time had passed since Emperor Antoninus's last visit to Bet She'arim, where Judah ha-Nasi lived.

I'll surprise Rabbi Judah with a visit today, thought Antoninus, and hear how he has been these past few months.

When Antoninus knocked on Judah ha-Nasi's door, the Rabbi and his family were enjoying their Sabbath meal.

Rabbi Judah embraced his friend. "What an honor this is, Emperor. Come in. Have you eaten?"

Antoninus joined the family at the table laden with bread and meat, fruit, and wine. The food was cold because no cooking was permitted on the Sabbath. But everything tasted delicious and Antoninus enjoyed himself enormously. He tasted this and drank that, singing and talking in between courses.

"I have never tasted any food so delicious," Antoninus said to his host.

"You must come back tomorrow," said Rabbi Judah, "and eat with us again. You have been away too long."

So Antoninus came back to Rabbi Judah's house for dinner the very next day.

This time the dishes were steaming hot, since it was no longer

the Sabbath and cooking was permitted. The bread was warm from the oven, the meat and side dishes hot from the fire.

Emperor Antoninus tasted of this and drank of that, yet he ate only half the amount of food he had eaten the night before.

"Is there something wrong?" asked Rabbi Judah, who was always careful to see after his friend's needs.

"Rabbi Judah," Antoninus said, "the food is good. But even though it is hot, it is not as tasty as yesterday's. Perhaps your cook forgot something, a spice she used before."

At first Rabbi Judah looked puzzled. He tasted his meat and then he nodded. "You are right," he said. "There is one spice missing."

"Well, if you are lacking something," said Antoninus, "please tell me and I can have it brought from the royal kitchens for you."

"No," said Rabbi Judah. "This spice cannot be found in the royal kitchens."

"Then tell me its name and I will have my steward buy it for you at the marketplace, or my traders can bring it from afar."

"No," said Rabbi Judah. "This ingredient cannot be bought at the marketplace or brought from a foreign land. It is called the Sabbath spice and it can only be found in food served on the Sabbath day. For when people take delight in the holy day, their food is spiced with the special flavors of observance, love, and joy."

Midrash Rabbah Genesis 11:4
Shabbat 119a

Rabbi Joshua and the Messiah

R abbi Joshua ben Levi was a great teacher and scholar. Because of his merit, it is said that he was privileged to visit the Garden of Eden, and that he even studied with the Prophet Elijah.

Often, Rabbi Joshua would ask the great Prophet questions that burned in his mind.

"I pray for the coming of the Messiah each day," he told Elijah. "I long to see this descendant of King David bring God's message to the people. And I long to see the people turn to God's ways of righteousness and justice. I pray and I wait, but I do not know when he will come."

"Go and ask him then," the Prophet answered.

"But I do not know where to find him," said Rabbi Joshua. "Is he really so near?"

"You will find him sitting at the city gate," said Elijah.

"The city gate!" exclaimed Rabbi Joshua. "There are so many people at the city gate. How will I know the Messiah from all of these?"

"He will be among the lepers," said Elijah. "You will watch the others untie all their bandages at once, clean their sores, and then retie all the bandages once again.

"The Messiah will be the only one who will untie one bandage at a time, wash the sore, and retie that bandage before going on to the next one. He wants to be ready every moment in case he is needed to bring God's message."

Rabbi Joshua thanked Elijah and immediately went to the city gate. He looked all about him at the people coming and going, sitting and chatting, and begging for food. Rabbi Joshua usually liked the noise and busyness of the gate but today it irritated him. He had one purpose only—to find the man who bandaged his sores one at a time.

When he located the lepers, Rabbi Joshua stood watching first one and then another. Just as the Prophet had said, nearly all of them first removed all their bandages, washed their sores, and then retied all their bandages. But there was one who was different, who treated just one sore at a time.

Rabbi Joshua walked over to this one.

"Peace upon you, Master and Teacher," Rabbi Joshua greeted him.

"Peace upon you, son of Levi," the man answered, this man who looked like all other men, but was not like them.

"Master, I have prayed for your coming each day," explained Rabbi Joshua. "I wonder when you will come to bring God's message of peace."

"Today," the Messiah answered.

Rabbi Joshua was stunned. Today? This very day? He could not believe what he had just heard! The time of peace and God's glory were to begin today!

"We are in such need of you," said Rabbi Joshua excitedly. "Thank you."

Rabbi Joshua left the city gate to tell all his students, family, and friends to prepare for the end of days, the days of peace and enlightenment.

At his House of Study, he prayed with his fellow scholars, discussed Torah, and waited. With each passing hour, however, his excitement diminished. He began to grow impatient.

Finally, in the middle of the night, Rabbi Joshua reached despair. He left the House of Study to search for Elijah. He found him, as he often did, at the tomb of the great sage Shimon bar Yohai.

"I spoke to the Messiah at the city gate," Rabbi Joshua began.

"Yes?" said Elijah.

"He said he would come today."

Elijah nodded.

"Today is over," continued the Rabbi. "And he has not come. He spoke falsely to me."

"Oh, I see," replied Elijah. "You don't understand. When he said it would be today, he was quoting from a psalm. The whole line from that psalm says, 'Today, if you will hear God's voice.'

"What he meant was that on the day the people hear God's voice and adhere to God's ways, the Messiah will come. He will bring the days of peace and joy to all mankind."

Rabbi Joshua thought for a moment. "I think that now when I pray for the Messiah to come," he said aloud, "I will add something to my prayer."

"What is that?" asked Elijah.

"I will pray for the coming of the Messiah just as I have always done, but I will also pray that the people listen to God's voice and cling to God's ways. In that way, they will be partners in bringing the Messiah and the days when God's holiness will fill the earth."

Sanhedrin 98a

The Pious Cow

Eliezer's cow was strong and healthy and a very good worker. Every day she pulled his plow through the fields—every day except the Sabbath. For Eliezer was Jewish and rested on the seventh day. His animals rested too.

Eliezer and his cow worked hard together for many years. But after several meager harvests, Eliezer became poor and was forced to sell his possessions, including his beloved cow.

During the first few days, the cow worked hard for her new master, just as she had for Eliezer. But her new owner did not observe the Jewish customs and when it came to the seventh day, he did not rest as Eliezer had. He worked every day, one day being just like another.

When the Sabbath came, the new owner tried to hitch the cow to his plough, but she would not budge. He yelled commands to her. "Go! Forward! Go!" Still she would not budge. Then he beat her angrily with his whip. The cow did not move.

The new owner ran to Eliezer's house. "What kind of a cow did you sell me? She won't work. She won't even get up. I want all my money back. Every bit of it."

"I don't understand," said Eliezer. "She was always such a good worker. Wait. Did she work yesterday?"

"Yes, she did," admitted the new owner.

"And the day before?" Eliezer asked.

"Yes. But she won't even get up today."

"Take me to her," said Eliezer.

The two men walked over to the field where the cow lay resting, chewing some grass.

"See what I mean?" said the new owner, pointing to the cow. "Now does she look like a good worker to you?"

Eliezer bent down and whispered something into the cow's ear.

Soon the cow was up, ready to work. Her new owner could not believe the change.

"What did you say to her?" he asked.

"I told her that when she belonged to me, we all rested on the Sabbath, as God commanded. But now she belongs to a new master

who isn't Jewish, and who does not rest on the Sabbath. So she must work also, as does her master."

The new owner grew thoughtful. "This animal has learned to keep the rest day while I, a human, work seven days with no rest and no knowledge of my Creator. I believe I will follow your cow's lead," he said to Eliezer.

He took the cow back to the barn and did no more work that day or on the other Sabbath days to come. Soon he began to study the Jewish laws and not only became a Jew, but a rabbi as well. He was known as Rabbi Hanina ben Torta, Rabbi Hanina, son of the cow.

Midrash Aseret Hadibrot
Pesikta Rabbati, chap. 14

One More Try

There had been one storm after another and the merchant ship had been blown off course. Now it would be many days before it could dock and replenish its supplies.

The captain was worried and called for his cook. They had worked many years together, and he had come to trust the cook not only for his services, but also for his advice.

"I know we do not have enough food for the whole crew and our passengers for the rest of the journey," said the captain.

"I thought of that myself, sir," answered the cook.

"I thought I would ask that merchant for help, the one who carries dried dates and figs and olives in oil from the Holy Land."

"That miser?" grumbled the cook. "He would not give us the pit of an olive if we asked him, sir. He will watch us grow thin while he enjoys his wares."

"I will try anyway," said the captain. "He must have some feeling in his heart for others."

The captain approached the merchant that evening before dinner.

"I have a favor to ask you, sir," the captain began. "Because of the storm, our journey will take much longer than we planned. We are in need of food for our passengers and crew. Perhaps you would share some of your fruit with us at a reasonable price."

"Humph," snorted the merchant. "Not when I can get a large sum when we dock. What do you take me for, Captain, a fool?"

The captain could see he would get nowhere with this selfish man. He went to the kitchen to tell the cook he was right.

"So there is nothing to do but make what we have last longer," said the captain.

"Perhaps there is one more thing we could try," suggested the cook. "Yes," he smiled. "One more thing."

The cook waited before carrying out his plan, but he would not tell the captain what he was going to do. He only smiled when the captain questioned him. Then one day he beckoned the captain to follow him.

"It has been long enough," he said.

The puzzled captain followed his cook to the merchant's cabin. Knock knock.

The merchant opened his door. He frowned.

"What is it this time? I hope it is not about the goods that I carry, for I have not changed my mind about giving you some."

"Come with me," said the cook. "I have something to show you."

The cook led the merchant and the captain to the ship's hold. Boxes filled with cloth and beads, clay pots, tools, rugs, and the merchant's dates and figs and olives were piled all around.

The cook took a borer from behind one of the boxes and began to cut into the wood of the ship's hold.

"What are you doing?" cried the merchant in alarm. "Have you lost your mind?"

"It is no matter to you," said the cook. "I am merely making a hole under my spot on the boat. Not under yours. I've decided to die now rather than wait and starve before we reach port."

"But . . . but . . . ," the merchant sputtered. "The water will come in and flood the ship for me as well. You must know that. I will die too."

"What happens to you and your part of the boat is of no concern to me," said the cook. "I must think only of myself." And he continued to drill deeper and deeper into the hold of the ship.

The merchant grew more and more agitated until he caught sight of a smile on the captain's face. All this time, the captain had stood back and watched the cook curiously.

"Is this a trick?" the merchant asked the captain. And then he understood.

"I see what you are trying to show me," said the merchant, much more humbly than before. "We all travel on the same ship. What affects you affects me as well. If you drown, I drown. If you and your crew are hungry and cannot sail this ship to port, then I am lost at sea as well. I cannot sail this ship alone."

He went over to one of the crates. "See what you can prepare with this," he told the cook as he handed him one jar of food after another.

Midrash Rabbah Leviticus 4:6

The Clever Thief

In a certain kingdom there was a ruler who believed strongly in the justice of his laws and in adhering strictly to them.

"A law is a law," he would say to his advisors. And he never allowed exceptions to be made when enforcing them.

One day, a beggar was caught in the palace kitchens stealing cheese and bread.

The King ordered him to be hanged, as this was the punishment for stealing.

"But I am so poor and hungry," explained the beggar. "And you, oh King, have so much. Surely there is a bit of cheese and bread to spare. I would have asked first. I am not a thief by nature. But no one was about. And the sight of the food there on the tray. . . ."

"Sorry. No exceptions," interrupted the King. "Take this thief to the gallows!"

"What a pity. What a pity," bemoaned the thief as he walked in front of the guard whose sword pointed him in the right direction. "Now my father's secret will die with me. I would gladly have shared it with the King before being hanged."

"Out with it," ordered the King's guard. "What secret?"

"If the King would but put a pomegranate seed in the ground, I could make it grow and bear fruit overnight. Such is the secret my father taught me."

The guard stopped walking. "Perhaps the King would like to know of this secret before you are hanged. Let us return to him."

The guard brought the thief back to the King's chambers and he told the King his secret.

The King was interested.

"Show me," he said, and ordered the guard to fetch a pomegranate seed from the palace gardener.

Accompanied by the King's officers, the King, the guard, and the poor beggar went out into the garden. There the beggar dug a hole for the seed, but he did not put the seed into the ground. Instead he stood up.

"I can work the magic after the seed is placed in the ground, but I cannot be the one to do it," said the beggar. "Only a person who has never stolen or taken anything that did not belong to him may plant the seed. Since I am a thief, I need one of you to do the planting."

The group standing around the thief became silent, and in the silence birds' songs and insects' buzzing seemed to grow louder.

The thief turned to the Grand Vizier and held out the pomegranate seed in the palm of his hand.

"Would you do the planting?" the beggar asked.

The Grand Vizier was visibly shaken. "It will not grow if I plant it either," he admitted, "for once when I was a lad, I stole a small carving knife from my neighbor's house." He could not look at the thief directly, but lowered his eyes.

So the thief turned to the keeper of the King's books.

"Perhaps you would do the planting?" the thief asked.

It was the bookkeeper's turn to grow pale and bow his head.

"I cannot do this either," he said, "for I deal with sums of money each day. Perhaps there has been a day where I made a mistake and subtracted too much for the sums."

Each of the King's advisors as well as the King's guard admitted that he could not plant the seed.

"Then it must be you, oh King, who will plant this seed," said the thief, "for you are the only one here who has never taken anything that was not his."

The King's usually haughty features softened, and his straight shoulders slumped a little.

"Children can be attracted to pretty objects," the King began. "I remember a time as a child where I was severely punished for desiring my father's royal necklace and hiding it in my room. I did not know its value or importance. I only knew that its jewels shone

· 93 ·

like stars and sent rainbows running through my room when I held it in the sunlight by my window."

There was another silence after the King spoke, until the thief, still holding the seed, said, "You are all so mighty and powerful and want for nothing. Yet not one of you can plant this seed. While I, who stole a little food to keep from starving, am about to be hanged."

"You are a clever one," said the King, "to show us that not one of us is perfect. Should my laws be as strictly enforced as I wished them to be, none of us would be standing here today. I therefore revoke your punishment. You may go free. And in appreciation for the lesson you have taught me, I give you my father's necklace. Go, knowing that because of you, my laws will be forever enforced with compassion as well as justice."

Exempla of the Rabbis #433, p. 169

The Will

Awealthy merchant needed to travel to a distant country for his business. He left his son in Jerusalem to study Torah, and took his slave and his goods with him.

While he was away, the merchant became ill. As his illness grew worse, he could sense that death was near. What troubled him the most was the thought that his slave might take his money and goods and run off with them, leaving his son in poverty in Jerusalem. After all, freedom and riches were a great temptation, and his slave was not the most trustworthy of men.

He called his slave to him. "Fetch a scribe who knows how to transcribe wills," he said. "I do not have long to live, and must take care of my property."

The slave ran to the marketplace where the scribes sat and worked. Even though his master was dying, the slave felt a certain excitement.

Perhaps when my master dies, I can run away and act as a freeman, he thought. And if I take his goods, who's to know where I am or what I did? His son and friends are far away in Jerusalem.

Soon the slave returned with the scribe. The merchant could

not sit up in bed, but he was able to say to the scribe, "I give everything I possess to my slave. To my son I give one possession that is to be of his own choosing."

The slave was very surprised and much pleased. My master must think of me as his own son, he thought. Now I will be able to return to Jerusalem and live as a rich man.

He swore agreement to the will and thanked the merchant.

After his master's death, the slave hurried back to Jerusalem with the will and all of the goods.

He looked for the son and found him in the House of Study.

"Your father has died and this is his will." He held up the document signed by the merchant and sealed by the scribe. "I get everything," he boasted. "He left you only one thing of your choosing. Will it be a golden goblet or a precious stone?" He chuckled and turned away.

The son could not believe that his father had signed this will.

What have I done to lose my father's love? he asked himself. Why did he leave me only one object from all his possessions? What am I to do?

The son went to see his rabbi. He told him of his father's death and of the strange will.

"I am to choose only one possession from my father's entire fortune as my inheritance," he explained, sadness showing in his eyes.

The rabbi looked at his student and smiled. "Your father was a wise man and he knew his slave well," he said.

"But . . . but . . . ." The son felt more confused than ever.

"Let me explain. Then I will tell you what you are to do when you go before the court of law tomorrow," said the rabbi.

On the following morning, the rabbis of the court established that the will was genuine and would be upheld. The head of the court looked at the merchant's son. "You are to choose something from your father's estate," he said. "The rest will belong to your father's slave."

At that, the son walked over to the slave and put his hand on the slave's shoulder.

"For my one thing, I choose my father's slave," he said.

The slave was speechless. How could this be?

The judges ruled that since the son had chosen the slave as his one possession, all that the slave owned was his. And so they ruled that all of his father's wealth was now his.

Yalkut Shimoni, Kohelet 2:968

The Best Merchandise

A ship full of merchants set sail to a faraway land. The merchants talked all day and into the night about the goods they had brought to sell and how rich they would be when they had done so.

One man with a scroll just listened and read.

"What goods have you brought to sell?" he was asked.

"I cannot show my goods to you," he replied. "Yet I carry them with me always."

The others began laughing. "No silks or jewels? No dishes or vessels of oil or wine to show us? A fine fortune you will make," they teased. "What kind of a merchant are you?"

For days the other passengers joked about this merchant who had no goods to show.

Then one night, in the dark, a strange ship pulled alongside them.

The passengers watched in horror as ropes were flung across to their ship and dozens of fierce pirates climbed aboard. Knives and swords whipped through the air. Shouts and cries replaced the jokes and leisurely talk of the long voyage.

The pirates carried away all the bundles of cloth, the jugs of oil and wine, and the jewels and fine dishes, leaving the merchants with nothing.

When the ship finally docked at the faraway port, the merchants set foot onto land without a penny.

Some of the merchants decided to seek out the House of Study. Surely they would get help there, perhaps a meal or a place to sleep, a coin or two, or some work. Among them was the quiet man they had teased during the voyage.

As they entered the House of Study, they saw a group of men seated around a table, having a lively debate over a difficult passage in the Talmud.

The man who had traveled without any goods joined the discussion. He answered one question, then another. He knew what was contained in the Torah and the commentaries. He knew what the rabbis had said about this matter and that. All those listening grew to admire the stranger's knowledge and wisdom.

"Come with me this evening," said one man at the table.

"We would enjoy your company at dinner," said another.

"It would please us if you would be our rabbi," said a third. "Our community is in need of a scholar, a teacher, a leader such as yourself."

The merchants, who stood near the doorway of the House of Study, were amazed.

"We did not know you were a scholar," said one of the merchants. "Please forgive us, and ask these people to help us as well, for we have nothing left."

"Certainly, I will ask them," answered the scholar. "But remember, as I told you on the ship, I cannot show my goods to you. They are not in baskets or crates, or in bundles or vessels. But I carry them with me always. My goods are my years of study and the knowledge and wisdom I have acquired. You see from what happened on our voyage that the study of Torah is by far the best merchandise one can carry."

Midrash Tanhuma, Trumah 1:2

Leviathan and Fox

The fox is a shrewd animal. Even the great sea creature, Leviathan, had heard tales of how smart Fox was.

Leviathan wanted to capture Fox and eat his heart, which was said to contain Fox's wisdom. Leviathan sent his most powerful fishes after Fox.

"Bring Fox to me," commanded Leviathan. "Even if you must trick him."

The fish swam from the sea to the river that led to Fox's home. They could see him lying in the sun on the shore. When Fox spotted all the fish so close, his stomach began to growl. They would make a tasty meal, he thought, and ambled closer to the riverbank.

"Follow us," called one of the fish. "We will feed you whatever your heart desires."

Fox stood firmly on the shore. "I am a land creature," he answered wisely.

"Do you realize how much the sea creatures honor you?" asked another fish who knew that besides being smart, Fox was also vain. "Leviathan is dying and wants to name you his successor because of your wisdom and understanding. Come with us today."

The fish could see that Fox was interested by the way he came closer to peer at them. His smirk was gone, replaced by a look of interest.

"Jump onto one of our backs and you will be safe in the water," the second fish said. "We will carry you to Leviathan's throne where you will rule over the sea and its creatures all your life. You will have no need to search for food, as it will be brought to you. And you will have no fear of larger animals coming to prey upon you."

Fox imagined himself on Leviathan's throne.

I *am* very wise, he thought. Of course Leviathan would want to make me ruler after him.

So Fox jumped on the back of the largest fish.

As the fish swam through the water, Fox began to regret his decision. He felt uneasy. What am I doing in the river, he thought, when my home is on the land?

Fox suspected that just as he had played tricks on others in the past, these fish were now playing a trick on him.

"Since I am in your power," said Fox to the fish, "tell me the truth. Why are you bringing me to Leviathan?"

The fish hesitated to answer. But since Fox could not get away, they told him the truth.

"Leviathan wants to eat your heart so he will be as wise as you are," they said.

"You should have told me the truth at once," said Fox, looking genuinely concerned. "Now you will surely be punished when Leviathan finds you have brought me without my heart. Like all foxes when they go on a journey, I left my heart at home for safekeeping."

The fish stopped swimming immediately.

"What shall we do?" they whispered among themselves.

"Leviathan may eat us if we do not return with Fox's heart," said one fish.

"Bring me to the shore," suggested Fox. "I will fetch my heart and return to you. Then Leviathan can honor you, and me as well."

And so it was that the fish returned Fox to the very same spot on the shore. As they approached the riverbank, Fox jumped onto land as fast as he could and then began to laugh out loud at the fish.

"You fools. Whoever saw a creature travel without his heart? My heart was right here all the time." Fox thumped on his chest and jumped up and down in delight.

With great fear, the fish returned to their ruler, Leviathan, and told him their tale.

"Fox is indeed a shrewd animal," said Leviathan. "And you, fish, are fools."

Alphabet of Ben Sira 27a–28b, 36a

A Man of Good Deeds

There was a certain butcher who became wealthy through attention and hard work. But he was also a man of good deeds. Every Friday before Shabbat, he distributed meat to the poor near his shop and also gave money to charity.

Because the butcher was such an honest and important man in the city, the governor authorized him to collect customs duty from the ships that docked in the city's harbor.

One day a ship came in and, as usual, the butcher selected something from its cargo as duty payment. As he was leaving the ship, however, the captain stopped him.

"I have something to sell you, but I cannot tell you what it is," the captain said in a whisper. "What I can tell you, though, is that I have heard of your reputation and I know that you, of all people, will be very interested in this merchandise."

"You expect me to buy something when I don't even know what it is? I never heard of such a thing," answered the butcher, and brushed past the captain, whom he considered sly and troublesome.

The captain grabbed his shirt. "Believe me. You will be very sorry if you do not purchase my merchandise—10,000 pieces of gold and it will be yours."

The butcher hesitated. There was something compelling in the captain's voice. "Show me this merchandise first and let me decide."

"No. You must buy it without seeing it. But now it will cost 20,000 pieces of gold," said the captain.

Even though the butcher did not trust the captain, he wondered if he should buy the merchandise. It was only money he would pay, after all. Yet 20,000 pieces of gold was a lot of money.

"You will regret it if you do not," said the captain.

"All right, 20,000 pieces," agreed the butcher reluctantly. "And this better not be a trick."

"It is no trick. But the price is now 40,000 pieces," said the captain. "It will be worth that much to you."

"Forty thousand in gold!" The butcher exploded with anger. "What do you make of me? A fool?" Yet a strange feeling inside him said, pay the money. So he went home to get the coins.

He gave them to the captain and watched as the man climbed down into the hold of the ship. Had he indeed made a fool of himself by allowing the captain to play games with him? He would soon find out.

He heard noises coming from the hold, low muffled sounds as if a whole flock of sheep were climbing the stairs and their shepherds were shouting for them to move along. Could he have purchased a flock of sheep? Forty thousand gold coins was a lot to pay for a flock of sheep.

Then the door to the hold opened. An old woman crawled out. She had no teeth and her clothes were all torn. Next a man came out carrying a baby. Both were thin from hunger and pale from lack of sun.

The butcher watched mesmerized as one person after another emerged from the ship's hold. Young and old. Clothed and unclothed. Crying and serious. All were thin, and fear filled their eyes.

"This is your merchandise," said the captain. "Two hundred Jewish souls we captured and hoped to sell as slaves. But they grew so thin and ill on the journey that no one would buy them. If you had not paid for them today, I would have flung them into the sea."

The butcher was furious at the captain's cruel words and determined that as soon as he got the captives off the ship, he would tell the governor about this captain and his crew.

He led the captives off the ship and to his home where he and his servants fed them and gave them clothing and beds to sleep on. He found them homes and work in the city and saw that they were settled there.

Among the captives was one especially beautiful, sweet young woman. The butcher thought she would make a wonderful wife for his only son, who agreed to the match. The woman seemed a bit reluctant, however.

Perhaps she is shy or modest, thought the butcher, and told her that his home and all his wealth would be hers if she married his son. She agreed to the match.

It was a big wedding. There was much food, many people, and musicians everywhere playing and singing. All the former captives had been invited and each looked healthy and strong.

Still, the young woman seemed sad, not happy and bright as a bride should be. The butcher was worried. What could have gone wrong with his good deed? He meant to give this captive a husband, a home, and riches.

Absentmindedly, he walked through the crowd listening to the banter, the laughter, and the songs. But through the joyful noises, he caught the sound of someone crying. He followed the sound and saw a young man crouched on the floor weeping.

"Why do you weep at a wedding?" asked the butcher.

"I cannot tell you," said the young man.

"But you must," insisted the butcher.

The young man looked up. "You saved my life. You saved all our lives. We owe you so much that your son's bride and I could not tell you we were engaged to be married when the pirates ransacked our village and carried us away. Your son's bride was to be my bride. That is why I cry."

The butcher was silent. "I will go talk to my son," he said finally. "Fortunately, the marriage vows have not yet been spoken."

When the butcher told his son the young man's story, his son released his bride so she could marry the youth from her village.

"She has suffered enough sorrow as a captive," his son said. "Let her marry her love."

So the butcher's son stepped aside and the two captives were wed, the young woman smiling brightly as a bride should. The couple thanked the butcher and his son not only for freeing them and saving their lives, but for allowing them to marry as well.

The butcher was content to know that, indeed, he had not been a fool, but had been guided by the Holy One to perform great deeds in his lifetime. He had been fortunate not only in redeeming captives about to die, but also in bringing together a man and a woman who had been torn apart.

"Blessed be the Ever Present One," whispered the butcher. And he joined in the feasting and merriment around him.

Yalkut Sippurim III, p. 106

The Brothers
of Ashkelon

Two brothers bought land in the city of Ashkelon and worked hard to produce crops. They built a fine house and prospered. They yearned for the time that they would be able to leave their farm for a short pilgrimage to the Holy City to pray at the Temple.

"This Passover let's go to Jerusalem and celebrate the holiday with our people there," said one brother. "Then we could sacrifice the purest white lamb at God's altar."

"Yes. It's time," said the other brother. "But we can't leave our house and lands unattended."

"We can ask our neighbor to watch our property for us," said the first brother. "Even though he is an idol-worshiper, he is friendly toward us."

Their neighbor seemed pleased to help the brothers, and so they told him of their plans to leave the next day.

The brothers did not know that their neighbor had grown jealous over the years as he watched them work and prosper. Now, with the brothers gone, he could at last put his plan into action. He would take what he wanted from them and invent a story about a band of thieves passing through the city.

The next morning, the two brothers awoke early, said their morning prayers, and in good spirits, headed for Jerusalem with their animals and baggage.

Their neighbor awoke later and strode over to the brothers' house. To his surprise, he saw the two brothers working in their fields.

Perhaps they were too afraid to leave their property in my care after all, he thought.

Each day when the neighbor looked at the brothers' house, he saw them working, going to and fro, smiling and waving.

Days passed and one evening there was a knock on the

neighbor's door. When he answered it, he saw the two brothers laden with packages.

"For you," said one brother.

"For watching our house and our lands while we were away," said the other.

"Everything is just as we left it," said the first.

"But, but . . . ," sputtered the neighbor. "You never left. You were here all the time."

The brothers looked questioningly at each other.

"We did leave. Just as we told you," said the first brother.

"We spent the Passover holiday in Jerusalem," said the other. "There were so many people there with their animals. No inn had an empty room. No house was without a guest."

The brothers showed their neighbor the cloth and baskets and jars they had brought for him.

"Then who did I see coming in and out of your house? Waving and smiling? Working in the fields?" the neighbor wondered aloud.

"Did the two men look just like us?" asked the first brother.

"Yes," answered the neighbor. He grew fearful as he looked at the gifts from the distant city and saw that the brothers had indeed been away.

"I cannot accept these gifts. Please forgive me." Their neighbor tried to control his quivering voice.

His hands shook as he covered his cheeks with them. "I planned to rob your house while you were away," he continued in a whisper. "Your God must have been watching over you."

Then the brothers understood. "Blessed is God Who looks after us," said the first brother, "and sends angels to guard us from evil."

"And know that we forgive you your evil thoughts," said the second brother to the neighbor. "Let us live in peace."

Midrash Rabbah Song of Songs 7:1

Glossary

Archangels. The seven angels who lead the world of angels and who have access to God's presence. They are Uriel, Raphael, Raguel, Michael, Sariel, Gabriel, and Jeremiel.

Alef-bet. The Hebrew alphabet.

C.E. Common Era. Instead of C.E., Christians use the term A.D., an abbreviation for anno Domini, the year of the Lord.

Circumcise. To cut off part or all of the foreskin of a baby boy's penis on the eighth day after birth. Circumcision is a sign of the covenant between God and the Israelites.

Hallah. A loaf of bread, often baked in the form of a braid or twist, eaten on the Sabbath and on various Jewish festival days.

Idol. An image of a deity, which is used as an object of worship.

Kosher. Generally, fit or proper. The word used to describe foods or ritual acts that are correct, faultless, and permitted within the framework of Jewish law.

Leper. A person who has leprosy, an infectious disease characterized by ulcerations, loss of fingers and toes, spots of excess skin pigment or loss of pigment, etc.

Leviathan. In the Bible, the leviathan is a multi-headed sea serpent, a legendary animal that will be prepared as part of the celestial meal for the righteous ones in the world to come.

Messiah. Anointed, chosen by God. In the tradition, the Messiah is a descendant of King David who will bring God's message and peace to the world.

Mishnah. The earliest portion of the Talmud, compiled by Rabbi Judah ha-Nasi about 200 C.E. It contains the Oral Law transmitted through the generations.

Nasi. An important person. In rabbinic times, Nasi was a title given to the president of the Sanhedrin, the high court of the land.

Pilgrimage. A journey, especially a long one, made to some sacred place as an act of devotion.

Rabbi. Title—meaning my master—for a sage. After the Middle Ages, the word *rabbi* came to mean a teacher, preacher, and spiritual head of a Jewish congregation, as well as an interpreter and decider of the law.

Rebbetzin. Yiddish for a rabbi's wife.

Rosh Hodesh. The monthly holiday of the New Moon.

Sabbath. Commemorates the seventh day when God rested after creating the world. Jews also rest on this day and abstain from work, enjoying a day of spiritual refreshment.

Sacrifice. An offering to God of animal or vegetable life, food, drink, or some precious object as a form of worship, of serving God.

Sanhedrin. The supreme political, religious, and judicial body in Israel during the Roman period and until about 425 C.E.

Shamir. In Jewish tradition, a legendary worm that was capable of splitting the hardest substance.

Shekinah. Dwelling or resting. Refers most often to God's presence in the world. Shekhinah was seen by the mystics as the feminine aspect of God.

Shema. The prayer "Hear, O Israel, the Lord our God, the Lord is One."

Talmud. The second most sacred Jewish text after the Bible, compiled from 200 B.C.E. to 500 C.E. A vast collection of rabbinic law, stories, thought, and commentaries on the Bible.

Tefillin. Phylacteries; two black leather boxes containing passages from Exodus and Deuteronomy. They are bound by black strips on the left hand and on the head, and are worn for morning services on all days of the year except Sabbaths and scriptural holy days.

Temple. In ancient Israel, the central building for the worship of God, located on Mount Moriah in Jerusalem.

Torah. Teaching. Often refers specifically to the Five Books of Moses as distinct from the rest of the Bible, which includes the Prophets and Writings. In a broader sense, Torah refers to the whole of the Bible and the Oral Law.

Tzaddik (pl. **tzaddikim**). An unusually righteous person.

Tzedaka. Righteous action toward those in need; charity.

Zealots. Jewish resistance fighters who seized the Temple in 66 C.E. and fought the Romans. They followed the principles of Judah the Galilean, that the Jews should not pay tribute to Rome or acknowledge the emperor, a mortal man, as their master.

Bibliography

Adelman, P. V. (1986). *Miriam's Well: Rituals for Jewish Women Around the Year.* Fresh Meadows, NY: Biblio Press.

The Babylonian Talmud (1938). Trans. Rabbi I. Epstein. London: Soncino.

Braude, W. G., trans. (1959). *The Midrash on Psalms.* New Haven, CT: Yale University Press.

Chanover, H., ed. (1985). *Home Start.* New York: Behrman House.

Cherry, K. (1972). *Lessons from Our Living Past.* New York: Behrman House.

Encyclopedia Judaica (1972). New York: Macmillan.

Feldbrand, S. (1980). *From Sarah to Sarah.* Brooklyn, NY: Eishes Chayil Books.

Frankel, E. (1989). *The Classic Tales: 4,000 Years of Jewish Lore.* Northvale, NJ: Jason Aronson.

Freehof, L. (1988). *Bible Legends: An Introduction to Midrash.* New York: UAHC Press.

Gaster, M. (1968). *The Exempla of the Rabbis.* New York: KTAV.

——— (1981). *Ma'aseh Book: Book of Jewish Tales and Legends Translated from the Judeo-German.* Philadelphia: Jewish Publication Society of America.

Gerlitz, M. (1980). *In Our Father's Ways.* Jerusalem, Israel: Oraysoh Publishers.

Ginzberg, L. (1988). *Legends of the Jews.* Philadelphia: Jewish Publication Society of America.

Harlow, J., ed. (1979). *Exploring Our Living Past.* New York: Behrman House.

Hauptman, J. (1974). Images of women in the Talmud. In *Religion and Sexism*, ed. R. Ruether, pp. 196–210. New York: Simon & Schuster.

Henry, S., and Taitz, E. (1988). *Written Out of History: Our Jewish Foremothers*. Fresh Meadows, NY: Biblio Press.

Marenof, M. (1969). *Stories Around the Year*. Detroit: Dot Publications.

Midrash Rabbah (1983). Trans. Rabbi H. Freedman: New York: Soncino.

Mimekor Yisrael: Classical Jewish Folktales (1976). Coll. M. J. bin Gorion, ed. E. bin Gorion, trans. I. M. Lask. Bloomington: Indiana University Press.

Patai, R., trans. (1988). *Gates to the Old City: A Book of Jewish Legends*. Northvale, NJ: Jason Aronson.

Pirke de Rabbi Eliezer (1965). Trans. and annot. G. Friedlander. New York: Herman Press.

Prose, F. (1974). *Stories from Our Living Past*. New York: Behrman House.

Segal, Y. (1976). *Our Sages Showed the Way*. New York: Feldheim.

Serwer-Bernstein, B. (1987). *Let's Steal the Moon*. New York: Shapolsky.

Taylor, S. (1980). *Danny Loves a Holiday*. New York: Dutton.

Weissman, R. M. (1980). *The Midrash Says*. New York: Benei Yakov Publications.

——— (1986). *The Little Midrash Says*. New York: Benei Yakov Publications.

About the Author

Barbara Diamond Goldin currently teaches language arts to middle school students at Heritage Academy in Long Meadow, Massachusetts. She is the author of eleven children's books, including *Night Lights: A Sukkot Story*; nonfiction such as *Bat Mitzvah: A Jewish Girl's Coming of Age*; historical fiction such as *Fire: The Beginnings of the Labor Movement*; and collections of stories, including *Creating Angels: Stories of* Tzedakah. Her books have received such awards and recognition as the National Jewish Book Award (for *Just Enough Is Plenty: A Hanukkah Tale*); the Sydney Taylor Picture Book Award (for *Cakes and Miracles: A Purim Tale*); and the American Library Association Notable Book Award for 1995 (for *The Passover Journey: A Seder Companion*). She lives in western Massachusetts with her two children.